The Family
Love It and Leave It

TONY HUMPHREYS BA, HDE, MA, PhD

D1146983

GILL & MACMILLAN

Gill & Macmillan Ltd
Goldenbridge
Dublin 8
with associated companies throughout the world
© Tony Humphreys 1994, 1996
0 7171 2490 8

Index compiled by Helen Litton
Print origination by
Carrigboy Typesetting Services, Co. Cork
Printed by ColourBooks Ltd, Dublin

A catalogue record is available for this book from the British Library.

1 3 5 4 2

For my own family
Jack, Kintha, Marie, Bobby and Paul

ACKNOWLEDGMENTS

The people who have most influenced the writing of this book are my own family and the many families I have worked with over the last twenty years.

I want to lovingly acknowledge the contribution of my partner in life Helen, who was a tremendous source of encouragement and support.

Special thanks to John and Pat Ryan for their enthusiasm and valuable comments and feedback.

CONTENTS

INTRODUCTION

The concept of what constitutes a family is no longer clear-cut. Traditionally, the family was defined as comprising mother, father and children. However, lone-parent families are now a common and an ever-increasing phenomenon. There are also families where the parents are a homosexual rather than a heterosexual couple. We are living in an era where between one in four and one in two marriages in Western countries break down. Typically, marital conflict and breakdown have profound effects on family stability. We are also in an era where children are gaining more legal power and have a greater voice; we have even witnessed a case in America of a child divorcing parents who were neglectful. The ideas in this book apply to all kinds of families, not just the traditional kind.

Creating a family is a major responsibility and one not to be lightly taken on. Prospective parents are not often prepared for the job of creating a family. Many parents forget that the family is as much there for their mature development as it is for that of their children. The responsibilities of creating a family are many and include such issues as:

- creating a separate family unit free of negative interference from outsiders
- where there is a couple, the creation of a couple relationship that is loving and supportive of each other's growth and development
- possession of basic parenting skills
- negotiation between parents on matters of family responsibilities
- development of a family atmosphere of unconditional loving and valuing of each other
- resolution of couple and family problems
- development of the self-esteem of each family member
- meeting the needs of family members
- development of responsible behaviour in all members of the family

- creation of positive communication between members of the family
- development of self-reliance and independence in each family member.

Quite a tall order for any prospective parent! Nevertheless, that is the reality of creating a healthy family.

Chapter 1 encourages prospective parents, before embarking on creating a family, to look seriously at their reasons for doing so and to be aware of what such an undertaking entails. Chapter 1 further encourages prospective parents to check their own levels of self-esteem and the quality of the relationship with each other. If there are serious problems in either area family problems will almost certainly ensue.

In spite of the high rate of problematic families, it must be remembered that families always do their best, within the limitations of the level of self-esteem that the parents have inherited from their families of origin. However, once a family develops awareness of what makes for a happy family then change can be brought about. The enmeshed family is the most typical kind of problematic family and the means of recognising and changing this family are outlined in Chapter 2. The much sadder profile of the neglectful family is drawn in Chapter 3 along with guidelines on how to bring about positive change. Creating the loving family is the theme of Chapter 4 and many of the issues that arise here are expanded in Chapters 5–10: positive resolution of family conflict (Chapter 5); meeting the needs of family members (Chapter 6); making the most of family feelings (Chapter 7); communicating effectively within the family (Chapter 8); developing responsibility within the family (Chapter 9); and fostering individuality within the family (Chapter 10). The last chapter of the book is concerned with the ultimate measure of the effectiveness of the family – the ability of its members to leave as independent and separate individuals. This leaving is not just a physical exodus from the home but is much more an emotional leavetaking, wherein the young person sees herself, and is seen by other family members, as a person in her own right.

It is advisable to read the book through to get a sense of its overall theme. However, each chapter stands on its own and can be usefully referred to when a problem or a question arises within a particular area of family functioning. The book provides the reader with relevant family case-studies and offers tried and tested ways of achieving family harmony.

This book is aimed particularly at parents because they are the family architects but it has relevance for anybody interested in the area of family dynamics. It has special relevance for prospective parents as it provides insight into what is entailed in establishing a family. The book will also be of help to young adults who are struggling to find their own identities and are having difficulties in separating out from homes that are problematic. For professionals involved in helping unhappy families (for example, social workers, community nurses, psychiatric nurses, clinical psychologists, counsellors, school liaison officers, youth workers), the book will be a useful handbook for intervention. It could also be used by groups of parents to work through together the issues involved in creating happy families.

The book has evolved from my own family and life experiences and from my professional involvement with distressed families, couples, adults, adolescents and children. In my experience parents and other family members are always eager to provide a positive home life for each other but sometimes they are not aware of the blocks to family harmony and of how to overcome them. My hope is that this book will provide clear guidelines for the creation of happy families.

CHAPTER 1

Parents: The Family Architects

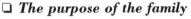

- ❑ **The purpose of the family**
  - ■ Parents always do their best
  - ■ Defining the family
- ❑ **Deciding to have a family**
  - ■ Essential questions for prospective parents
  - ■ Unwise reasons for having children
- ❑ **Blocks to the development of the happy family**
  - ■ Parents from troubled families of origin
  - ■ Self-esteem difficulties of parents
  - ■ Disharmonious couple relationship
  - ■ Adverse social and material circumstances
- ❑ **Basis of family harmony**
  - ■ Separation of parents from families of origin
  - ■ High self-esteem of parents
  - ■ Harmonious couple relationship
  - ■ Awareness of what makes for a happy family
  - ■ Favourable social and material circumstances
- ❑ **Freedom from outside family influences**

All human failures are the result of a lack of love.
Alfred Adler

❑ **The purpose of the family**

In this book the recommendations made for establishing happy families are based partly on the knowledge that has emerged in the fields of psychology and sociology over the last hundred years; they are also based on my own family experiences and my work with troubled families and individuals over the last twenty years. It is the emotional climate of the family that sets the scene for family harmony or disharmony. The purpose of

1

the family is to develop relationships that will create the fertile ground for each family member to mature into high self-esteem, independence and productivity.

I am a great believer in humankind. I believe we have immense capacity to do good for one another. I know that we have limitless potential to learn to be effective architects of family relationships. The pity is that many do not get the support and the opportunities to develop the knowledge and skills that lead to such effective relationships.

The purpose of a family is to provide for the optimum development of each person within that family. Too often, parents neglect their own development for the sake of the children's development, and, of course, sometimes the converse is true. Children need to be educated that parents also have needs and they, the children, can help their parents in their quest for fulfilment in life.

It is not too difficult to distinguish the effective family from the one that is ineffective. The effective family provides the loving, supportive and challenging environment for the total development of each member. The ineffective family creates an atmosphere wherein a poor sense of self, dependence and insecurity are developed. There are degrees of effectiveness and ineffectiveness and these are determined by the way families interact with and relate to one another in certain essential areas. The key areas that need to be considered and that are outlined in this book are:

- The ways of relating to each other (Chapters 2, 3 and 4)
- The type of loving shown (Chapter 4)
- How the family resolves conflict (Chapter 5)
- How needs are responded to (Chapter 6)
- How feelings are expressed and responded to (Chapter 7)
- The way the family communicates (Chapter 8)
- How family responsibilities are dealt with and allocated (Chapter 9)
- How the family provides for the development of the self-esteem of each member (Chapter 10)
- How the family responds when members leave the family (Chapter 11)

Parents are the architects of the family and my hope is that this book will provide the key knowledge and skills that are needed for this most important and creative emotional architecture. However, for parents to become the effective architects that I know they are capable of becoming, they must first look at their own internal architecture. Parents with high self-esteem are the most effective parents but the converse is also true.

■ Parents always do their best

When parents attend a course or read a book such as this, I am always concerned that they should hold on to a fundamental truth which is that parents always do their best. In my experience of helping troubled families, I have never yet come across a case where a parent deliberately neglected children or spouse. Certainly, unwitting neglect has been perpetrated and the consequences are often enormous for all family members (including the perpetrator). However, when parents manipulate, criticise, abuse and neglect their children or their spouses, this stems from their own abuse of themselves and from earlier abuse experiences in their own childhood. The fact that only a tiny minority of adults have high self-esteem indicates that the majority of people have experienced some level of neglect within their families of origin (and other social systems) and therefore it is not surprising that negative family patterns are repeated in newly created families. Parents as family architects are not then to blame for the unsound edifice they may build. But, they are responsible for the consequences of their actions. Once a parent is aware of neglectful patterns of behaviour then he is responsible for getting the kinds of help and learning that are needed to correct such neglect of self and family members. This is not a responsibility that a parent can be allowed to avoid. Too often a blind eye is turned to the abuse of spouses and children in our society. It is a blindness that has to stop because when it persists the victims of abuse themselves very often become the future perpetrators of abuse (either of self, of others or of property) and the sad vicious cycle of neglect is perpetuated.

■ Defining the family

What defines a family? Traditionally, a family was defined as mother, father plus children. In our modern pluralist society there are other models of family. For example, lone-parent families (occurring through choice, separation, divorce, death of spouse or desertion) now represent a sizeable group.

There is much controversy about the lone-parent family but it is a reality that has to be accommodated and not condemned from a questionable high moral ground. After all, the two-parent family has been responsible for much abuse and neglect. It is an unfounded assumption that a lone-parent family cannot be as effective as a two-parent one. In the area of marital break-down, research has shown that children are far better off with one happy parent rather than with two unhappy ones. What counts in creating an effective family is not the presence of two parents but the presence of a mature well-balanced adult. You could, for example, have a two-parent family where the father is dominant, aggressive and controlling and the mother is passive, dependent and non-assertive – the children of such parents hardly have a good model in either parent. Generally, a child identifies with either the father or the mother; in this example if the child identifies with the father she will take on the immature controlling characteristics of the father and if she identifies with the mother she will take on the mother's dependent behaviours. Either way, the child will not grow into a mature, self-motivated and constructive member of society.

What makes for a healthy family is not the gender issue of having a male and a female heading the family but the presence of a parent who has a balance of feminine and masculine characteristics. A single parent who is mature in terms of a balanced personality of masculinity and femininity will create a healthy family environment. Children do not necessarily need a father and a mother to jointly rear them but they do require at least one mature well-balanced person.

❏ *Deciding to have a family*

■ Essential questions for prospective parents

Parenting is the most difficult profession of all. In spite of the family being the core unit of our society, parenting remains largely an invisible profession. Research and experience have shown that most learning problems of children, problems of delinquency, criminal behaviour, violence and other abusive social behaviours can be traced back to the families of origin. There is a particular state in America which has invested heavily in training parents for the difficult task of creating effective families. This state has found that for every five dollars invested, twenty-five dollars have been saved later on remedial education costs, on costs arising from delinquency and criminal behaviour and on costs of psychological, social and medical services.

It is appalling that in our society no guidelines are given – by public education, counselling services or the churches – on the enormous responsibility and skills involved in creating a family where all members (parents as well as children) can become happy, productive and fulfilled individuals who are capable of unconditional love, understanding and constructive patterns of psychological and social behaviours.

In an attempt to provide a better chance for all in the family to be happy, mature and effective I would suggest that prospective parents consider whether they meet the following requirements before deciding to have a child:

- Ability to love, accept and value self
- Ability to unconditionally love and value another
- Ability to focus on the here and now
- Ability to communicate directly and clearly
- Ability to express and respond to feelings in oneself and in others
- Ability to be responsible for control of own behaviours and the ability to help children in consistent and positive ways to be responsible for themselves
- Ability to support and enhance the self-esteem of another
- Ability to cope with and resolve the inevitable family stresses that arise
- Ability to respect, value and meet the reasonable emotional, social, educational, creative, spiritual, physical, behavioural and independence needs of self, partner and children

If, as a prospective parent or as a current parent, you do not meet any one of these requirements, it is important that you set about resolving the area in which you feel you fall short. This book provides practical ways of developing the required personal, interpersonal and parental skills. What counts at this point is *awareness* of these goals and a *commitment to working towards attaining* them. You do not need to have reached your goals before embarking on having a family; if that were the case very few would be ready for parenting. Once you have knowledge of what makes for an effective family, then should you fail or lose control at some point it is not too difficult to correct the rift that has occurred in family relationships. Indeed, if you can admit vulnerability, apologise, and learn and grow from mistakes you will be a powerful model for other members of the family.

▪ Unwise reasons for having children

The most important reason for having a child is to give that child the opportunity of experiencing life in all its beauty, wonder and challenge. The child is not your possession. Your job is to provide the fertile family ground for a young child's unique development as a human being; in this way you as a parent give life to a child with no strings attached. If you bring a child into the world for any of the reasons outlined below, it is very unlikely that a healthy family environment will be created for that child. Some immature reasons for having a child which I have come across over the years include:

- My family or 'society' expects it
- To give meaning to my life
- To prove my manhood or womanhood
- To see if the child would look like me
- In order to save a failing marriage
- Because I have this 'cuddly' baby fantasy
- Gives me social status
- To tie my partner to me
- To have someone to look after me in old age
- To provide a companion for another child
- To give my child everything I never had

It may also be unwise to decide to have a child where resources are very overstretched or when one of the parents is irresponsible in terms of alcohol dependence, is violent, shows emotional and physical withdrawal, is non-communicative or is dismissive of and irritable with children. Clearly, when parents themselves have deep psychological and social problems such as depression, chronic anxiety and hallucinatory or delusional symptoms, or are unable to form close relationships, then a decision to have children must be postponed until these deep distresses are largely resolved.

❏ *Blocks to the development of the happy family*

Before looking at the positive steps that are needed to create a happy family it is necessary to outline the typical blocks to such a desirable process. These can be categorised usefully under the following headings:

- parents from troubled families of origin
- self-esteem difficulties of parents
- disharmonious couple relationship
- adverse social and material circumstances.

It is clear from these headings that parents are the crucial players within the family. The parents' own childhood experiences, their present feelings about themselves and the strength of their couple relationship are major factors that determine the well-being of their family.

■ Parents from troubled families of origin

Do you as a parent ever hear yourself say 'I sound just like my mother (or father)' or find yourself doing things in the same way as your father or mother? Do you find that your marriage relationship repeats that of your parents in certain ways? Maybe sometimes, during arguments with your partner, you shout 'you're just like your mother (or father)'. Perhaps, as a parent you find yourself repeating the negative patterns of irritability, ridiculing, scolding, comparing, threatening and so on that you experienced at the hands of your parents as a child? Or maybe you find yourself doing exactly the opposite from how your parents treated you – which can be just as problematic.

Unless you develop awareness the probability is that as a partner in a couple relationship and as a parent you will either repeat or directly oppose the patterns of relating that existed in your family of origin. This is not surprising for many reasons; for example, these are the patterns that are most familiar to you. However, I believe there are more profound reasons why such repeat patterns occur. A major purpose of repeat patterns is to get you as an adult to face unresolved issues from your childhood and to face the continuation of childish dependence in your adulthood. You are likely to marry a partner who resembles the parent who most negatively influenced you. In doing that you are faced once again with the negative aspects of your relationship with that parent. But now as an adult you have a chance to redeem yourself from the negative aspects of your partner's relationship with you. Likewise if as a parent you find yourself being overdemanding and critical of your child, you can redeem both yourself and your child from the consequences of such neglectful behaviours. An example will clarify these processes.

A frequently occurring relationship is where a man who is aggressive, dominant, critical and controlling marries a woman who is passive, people-pleasing, non-assertive and docile. In such a relationship the man may be like his father and have married a woman like his mother. The woman may be like her own mother and have married a man like her own father. Both parties in this newly formed relationship have come from problematic families of origin. It is unlikely that they will create a happy family. Why would this man choose to marry a woman like his mother who, after all, did not protect him against the wrath and abuse of his aggressive father? The purpose is threefold:

- to face his father within himself
- to face his mother within his wife
- to change the patterns of relating to self, partner, others and children.

This man's wife, who has chosen to marry someone like her father and who is herself like her own mother, is also faced with similar responsibilities:

- to face her mother within herself
- to face her father within her husband
- to change the patterns of relating to self, partner, others and children.

The man's first task is to face the father within himself. He has to stand back from his aggressive behaviours and ask himself: 'Why am I using these same means of relating to others as my father did in his relationship with me?' He needs to return to his childhood and witness again the effects of his father's behaviour on himself, on his mother and on other family members. He needs to feel the fear, hurt, humiliation, anger and helplessness that he experienced as a child so that he can be determined that he will not expose his children, himself and his partner to such sad experiences. Most of all, he needs to learn to love and care for himself in a way that both his parents were unable to do.

Likewise, the wife who is passive, timid and fearful needs to ask herself: 'Why am I as a grown-up adult using these same ways of relating to others as my mother did in her relationship with my father, with myself and others?' She too needs to return to her childhood and experience again the effects of her father's dominance and her mother's passive behaviours on her. She needs to see how she as a small child would have felt frightened, abandoned by both parents and helpless, and how she protected herself by being 'good' and passive (like her mother). Out of this understanding she can determine to let go of these protective passive ways, so that she as a mother does not abandon her children to a fate of being bullied and dominated or neglected because of passivity on her part. Like her spouse, she needs to become the positive parent towards herself that she missed in her own childhood.

Both the man and the woman also need to separate out from their own parents and to ensure that they are not continuing to be either dependent on them or controlled by them.

Separating out from parents does not mean not loving them but it does mean becoming independent of them.

Unless parents become aware of the enduring influence that troubled families can have on them, the danger is that the dependent and neglectful relationship patterns will be repeated in the newly formed family. Awareness is a prerequisite to change but unless it is coupled with determined, persistent alternative action that enhances family well-being then it will not bring about the desired change.

■ Self-esteem difficulties of parents

Your level of self-esteem is a critical factor in determining your effectiveness as a parent and the nature of your relationship with your partner.

Parents with high self-esteem have a deep sense of their worth, capability and value; they have a love of life; they express all their feelings and are not afraid to express their convictions; they have close relationships with each other and with relatives, friends and colleagues; they can accept constructive criticism, tolerate frustrations and see mistakes and failures as opportunities for further learning. Whilst being in touch with their strengths, parents with high self-esteem are also realistically aware of their weaknesses, shortcomings and lack of knowledge. They are true to themselves in their relationships with others and resist conforming to ways of being that are false or do not fit for them.

Parents with middle self-esteem have serious doubts about their acceptability and capability and are quite dependent on the approval of others, on appearances, on performance and on success for their sense of worth. Unsureness dogs their path at all times. Patterns of controlling and dominating or pleasing others figure frequently in their relationships with others. They have a fear of mistakes and failures and, consequently, they tend to play it safe in work, in social situations and in intimate relationships. They rarely feel satisfied and fulfilled in life.

Parents with low self-esteem have a deep sense of worthlessness and uselessness. They can be highly neglectful of self, of others or of both, and can be extremely difficult to please.

They are strongly self-critical and are hypersensitive to criticism. They can be either highly aggressive or extremely passive. They have huge difficulties in forming close relationships. In relationships they tend to be either possessive or dismissive. Any kind of challenge threatens them. They suffer from continual inner turmoil. Time and time again they unwittingly set themselves up for further hurt and rejection.

It is true that your childhood experiences determine your level of self-esteem. However, as a parent you cannot continue to blame the past for how you feel here in the present. If you do that you will remain 'stuck' in your bad feelings about yourself. You have the choice now, as an adult, to take responsibility for changing your level of self-esteem, to begin to heal the abuses of the past, so that you can relate in loving ways to yourself, your partner and your children and create a family life that is positively different from your own childhood experiences. Changing self-esteem is not an easy process; it demands constant work, but the rewards are great. Chapter 10 shows how the self-esteem of each member of the family can be enhanced. It is a good idea for parents to work as individuals, as well as a couple, on changing their own level of self-esteem. The process for doing that is outlined in my book, *Self-esteem: The Key to Your Child's Education*.

The important issue to bear in mind is that, whether you are aware of it or not, your level of self-esteem has a profound effect on the well-being of your family.

■ Disharmonious couple relationship

Individuals bring their self-esteem difficulties into the couple relationship and all the interactions between them are affected by their doubts, fears and insecurities. Parents are the leaders of the family, so when their relationship is troubled it is unlikely that they will be able to create a happy household.

The differences between partners can be challenging and exciting, and can be an opportunity to learn from each other. But in troubled couple relationships these differences become major sources of threat and can become the battleground on which each tries to establish control over the other. For instance, a partner who is aggressive will push that his needs, career, opinions and so on are more important than the other's, and the partner who succumbs to such pressures sacrifices her own individuality and independence. Neither parent in this case presents a good model of behaviour for children.

It is a sad fact that individuals with low self-esteem become involved with similarly troubled partners. It is also the case that people with high self-esteem marry partners like themselves as do people with middle self-esteem.

Troubled couple relationships are characterised by the regular occurrence of the following behaviours:

- Possessiveness
- Attempts at control
- Aggression
- Passivity
- Hypersensitivity to criticism
- Overinvolvement with each other
- Frequent need for reassurance
- Jealousy
- Frequent crying bouts
- Alcohol or drug dependence
- Reluctance to go out socially
- Shyness
- Sulking
- Frequent irritability
- Dominance
- Dismissiveness
- Violence
- Tirades
- Suicide threats
- Suicide attempts
- Emotional and physical withdrawal
- Silence that may go on for weeks or months
- Frequent emotional outbursts

Couple conflict does not inevitably lead to family problems. The ideal situation is where the couple resolve their difficulties, deepen their intimacy, establish their own individuality and maintain loving relationships with their children. If couples follow the guidelines given in this book for establishing a happy family they will also create a harmonious relationship with each other. However, they must be determined to resolve any difficulties that may arise between them so that both the couple and family relationships remain happily intact. If they are having difficulty in resolving their differences then it is wise to seek professional help.

Conflicting couples who stay together and whose children frequently witness 'scenes' between them have the most negative effect on family life. The next most damaging situation is where the conflicting couple separate but remain in conflict. When parents choose to separate, the optimum situation for the family is where the parting is friendly, where the parents, though now separated, befriend each other and where each maintains close loving relationships with the children. Because of the high rate of marital breakdown, the maintenance of family harmony following marital separation is a crucial issue. Couples must strive to prevent the differences between them or their separation leading to family breakdown as well.

■ Adverse social and material circumstances

Social problems such as poverty, unemployment, poor housing and overcrowding have an effect on family harmony. It is not the function of this book to address these sad and difficult circumstances, but it is necessary to recognise their influences. Clearly, in a family which is already troubled, the existence of unemployment, poor financial resources or poor housing are added pressures. Interestingly, the effects of unemployment and poverty on a close-knit family are minimal compared to the effects on a troubled family. In the harmonious family, support, understanding and an 'all for one and one for all' attitude operate in times of stress. Whatever the nature of the family, it is vital that financial difficulties are effectively and sensitively dealt with by government, social services and voluntary bodies.

Unemployment can have a huge impact on the self-esteem and on the social life of the unemployed person, and the need to create meaningful employment for this person is paramount. When the self-esteem of any member of the family is negatively affected, the well-being of the family becomes threatened. Lack of material resources also makes it harder for parents to create a caring, interesting and exciting home environment.

❏ *Basis of family harmony*

The means for developing a happy family are, in many ways, the opposite to the blocks to family happiness:

- separation of parents from families of origin
- high self-esteem of parents
- harmonious couple relationship
- awareness of what makes for a happy family
- favourable social and material circumstances.

▪ Separation of parents from families of origin

The function of the family is to bring each member to a position of emotional independence and to establish the capability of standing on one's own two feet. When parents continue to remain dependent on their own parents or look to others for approbation, they will not be able to set up their own family so that it is free from unwelcome interference by others. Non-separation from family of origin means that you maintain a childish and dependent mode in relationships – a mode which will be repeated in your relationships with your partner and your children. As a result, your family will become dysfunctional. It is essential therefore that you establish your separateness from your own parents so that you can pass on this independence to your family. (The issue of separation of parents from their families of origin is considered in detail in Chapter 11.)

▪ High self-esteem of parents

The qualities of the parent with high self-esteem have been outlined already. The parent with high self-esteem will effect similar levels in his children and will be effective in creating a harmonious family. Regrettably, high self-esteem is a rare phenomenon and there are few of us who do not need to work on elevating our sense of self. When parents' self-esteem is high the well-being of the family is ensured; however the converse is also true. As already mentioned, it is wise for partners to take individual responsibility for their own doubts about themselves while supporting and encouraging each other in the process of self-discovery. It is unwise for a parent to believe that the family will provide what is needed for self-esteem elevation. There are many adults who are genuinely loved by family members and others but whose own hate and rejection of themselves prevent them from internalising the love messages. Changing an adult's self-esteem primarily involves the creation of a loving relationship with oneself. The couple and family relationships can provide a supportive and encouraging environment for that process to occur but the major responsibility for change lies with the individual himself. Adults who are parents have an added responsibility to change how they relate to themselves because of the effect this has on their children and on their couple relationship.

■ Harmonious couple relationship

When parents relate well to each other the harmony spills over into family relationships but the converse is also true. The first responsibility for prospective parents and for couples already with children is to develop a positive regard for themselves. The second responsibility is to ensure that how they relate to each other acts as a positive model for all other relationships within the family. Children depend utterly on their parents and if they witness frequent conflict between them they become frightened and insecure. The recommendations throughout this book for creating effective family relationships equally apply to the couple relationship.

■ Awareness of what makes for a happy family

Parenting is the 'invisible profession'. There is no required training for it even though the responsibilities of parenting are enormous. Not only has one responsibility for oneself and for the couple relationship but also for the emotional, social, sexual, physical, educational, behavioural, creative and spiritual development of children. When parents lack knowledge of what makes for effective parenting they either resort to what their own parents did or do exactly the opposite. Either reaction may be detrimental to family well-being.

The *essential skills* that parents need to be aware of and to acquire in order to create a happy family are:

- Ability to recognise ways of relating that damage self-esteem and block family harmony
- Ability to form an unconditional loving relationship with each family member
- Ability to resolve problems that create family disharmony
- Ability to meet your own needs and to respond positively to the reasonable needs of family members
- Ability to positively express all feelings and to respond constructively to the expressed feelings of family members
- Ability to listen and communicate directly and clearly
- Ability to be responsible and to foster responsible behaviour in family members
- Ability to develop your own individuality and independence and that of family members
- Ability to withstand undue interference with the family from outside influences

The main purpose of this book is to outline the knowledge and the skills required to create an effective family. A once-off reading of the book is unlikely to be sufficient. What is required is regular practice of the ways of relating recommended in the book.

■ Favourable social and material circumstances

The need for favourable social and material circumstances as a basis for family harmony needs little elaboration. It is much easier to provide for emotional and other needs of the family when material resources are available and unemployment is not a factor. However, material resources and employment do not guarantee family happiness – quite the contrary in some cases. Materialism as a philosophy of life has not brought peace, serenity and contentment to human beings. The needs of human beings go far beyond material wealth.

❏ *Freedom from outside family influences*

A family needs to have a clear boundary around it that indicates 'we are a family unit that largely determines who we are, what we do and who we allow to cross the family threshold'. It is important that this boundary is not too rigid as a family needs advice, information, support and help from outsiders. However, the initiative for outside influence must come from the family. To tell a family what to do and how to be is a gross invasion of a family's privacy. Even when there are signs of unhappiness and neglect, while it is good that outsiders express concern and offer help, it is not wise to give unsolicited advice. However, if after such concern is shown children continue to be neglected, then this concern should be expressed to an agency that can take action to stop the neglect, encourage responsibility and provide the professional help that may be required to bring about desirable change.

The issue here is the undue influence of outsiders on the family, people who may exert a powerful negative influence on the functioning of the family, undermine the couple's relationship and damage the self-esteem of family members. The people who most commonly interfere with families are: in-laws (living with or outside the family), relatives, neighbours, friends and child-minders.

The live-in parents or the live-in in-laws are typical sources of negative influence on the family. These 'outsiders' may tell the young mother what to do and what not to do, they may expect her to be there at all times for them, they may interfere with the rearing of the children and they may weaken the couple relationship. I have worked with women who, on marrying, moved in with their in-laws and felt that they had no say in the running of the home. It is not wise, even when in-laws are positive and independent, to try to establish a new family under the roof of an existing family. It is a confusing three-generation situation, wherein the self-esteem of all can be so easily damaged. Birds need to fly the nest and build their own nests. A young couple need to have their own physical space to give them a chance of setting up an independent couple and family life. In a three-generation household the issue of 'who does what' can become a major source of contention. Privacy is more important than property: the chant that 'the house will be yours when we're gone' must not sway a young couple from finding their own space. The parents or in-laws may live another thirty to forty years and a young couple must not postpone their right to independence for any length of time, not to mind for so many years. Equally it is good for a young couple to remember that their parents survived without them before they were born. Protection of parents who are healthy and active only damages their self-esteem and maintains their dependence – hardly an act of caring!

Similarly, parents or in-laws outside the home can exert negative influences. I have worked with women whose mothers or mothers-in-law have a key to the young couple's family home and come and go as they please. This is not acceptable behaviour; the young couple need to assert their right to privacy and to be consulted before visits. There are fathers who expect their married sons or daughters to be on hand whenever they need them without consideration of whether or not it is convenient to do what is being requested. While young couples may want to respond to a parent's request, they must also be able to say 'no' when other priorities need their attention without creating an emotional storm. Moreover, they need to establish that commitments to themselves and their own children take priority.

Neighbours, aunts, uncles, friends and child-minders can also be major influences on family dynamics. There are parents who have great difficulty in saying 'no' to these people and they allow them to rule their couple life, boss their children and invade their homes as they please. These families are too open to outside influences and so children become confused, parents feel helpless and no sense of family unity and harmony is present.

Work can also unduly influence the family. The parent whose career takes up most of his free time neglects self, the couple relationship and the family. I have worked with many men who, later on in life, regretted not having spent time with their spouses and children. They have often felt hurt when their children as adults did not maintain contact, but the poor contact reflected what they gave to their sons and daughters when they were children. 'As you sow, so shall you reap.'

The task is clear: a young couple must ensure that outsiders or work or study does not lead to the neglect of family welfare or a loss of separateness as a family unit. In clear, firm and positive ways those who attempt to interfere must be told that, whilst they are loved and welcome in the home, they are not to interfere with the functioning of the family. When parents neglect these responsibilities, they neglect themselves and the family, and the consequence is a confusing, leaderless and unhappy family.

CHAPTER 2

Changing the Enmeshed Family

❏ *'Win at a cost' enmeshed family relationships*
- Narcissistic caring
- Overprotective caring

❏ *The web of enmeshed family relationships*
- Parents' relationship with one another
- Parents' relationships with the children
- Children's relationships with the parents
- Children's relationships with one another

❏ *Changing enmeshed family relationships*

*All happy families are alike, but each unhappy
family is unhappy in its own way.*
Leo Tolstoy

❏ *'Win at a cost' enmeshed family relationships*

'Win at a cost' enmeshed family relationships represent the
more typical ways that family members relate to each other.
These relationships are *conditional*: once a family member
measures up to the condition set by the other for gaining love
she is accepted by the other. However, the threat of withdrawal
of love and acceptance remains, and anxiety to please will dominate this relationship. For example, 'be good' is a common
condition for love within families and many children suffer
great hardship from being emotionally rejected over a small
misdemeanour. These children may become 'goodie-good'
children and later on 'people-pleasing' adults. The fear of being
rejected drives them further into anxiety to please. The 'cost'
is that independence, uniqueness, spontaneity, the right to one's
own opinions and the right to make mistakes are sacrificed in
order to gain affection, valuing and attention. In this family
each person's mature development is blocked. 'Win at a cost'

family relationships involve a giving to get and, depending on their nature and intensity, they breed multiple problems of low self-esteem, fear, depression and hopelessness among family members. These enmeshed relationships take two main forms:

- narcissistic caring
- overprotective caring.

▪ Narcissistic caring

Narcissistic caring is probably the most common form of relating found in families, classrooms and workplaces. It varies in degree and in intensity but the basic message in narcissistic relating is that 'you are there for me and once you meet my needs, see things my way, do as I tell you, believe what I believe, you will be accepted and loved'. It is conditional loving. Even though it can be highly neglectful, there is a way to gain recognition in the narcissistic family. It is a 'win' situation but at the 'cost' of sacrificing one's own uniqueness, individuality, freedom and independence. The parent who relates narcissistically is deeply insecure and believes that unless she ties the children to her they will not stay in the relationship. Such parents dominate and control children. Generally speaking, in a family where narcissistic relating prevails, one of the parents controls the scene. The aggressive dominating spouse, as already seen, is likely to marry a passive partner; this passive partner allows the other to control and has not got the security and the means to withstand the narcissistic behaviour of the partner. This marriage relationship is problematic from the start and this spills over into the creation of a problematic family.

It is important to see that dominance, controlling and oppression come from a need to be valued and accepted. In controlling the other members of the family, the dominant parent attempts to become secure through making the others totally dependent on her for all decision-making. But though spouse and children may acquiesce, they will also resent and have hidden feelings of anger towards this dominating family member. In many ways the parent who is insecure and relates narcissistically sets herself up for eventual rejection, the very thing she dreads.

The spouse may give the dominating partner the freedom to control but will spend as little time as possible in her company and will certainly not be spontaneous in showing affection, affirmation and acceptance. This increases the insecurity of the dominating parent, leading to an increase in controlling behaviour in order to ensure allegiance. What a sad vicious cycle!

If you go against the parent (or teacher or other significant adult in your life) who interacts narcissistically then the result is rejection, which can take many forms including:

- Severe criticism
- Blaming
- Labelling as 'useless', 'stupid', 'lazy', 'selfish'
- Prolonged hostile silences
- Violence
- Tirades
- Ridiculing
- Scolding
- Put-down messages
- Ranting and raving
- Shouting and roaring

All these reactions are an attempt to get you back into conforming to the narcissistic person's wishes, needs, convictions – whatever you have gone against. If you give in 'for peace sake' you will be accepted back with open arms but you are only going back into imprisonment. So many emotional crimes have occurred in families and schools under the banner 'for peace sake'. The narcissistic parent badly needs to be confronted by some strong secure person within the family. However, no such person exists in this kind of family and, therefore, the tyranny continues. Confrontation would benefit everybody in this family. It would help the parent who dominates by letting her know that 'you do not have to control me for me to love you'. It would help the passive partner by getting him to see that he is worthy of being loved and accepted for self and that he has every right to be different, unique and individual in the way he lives life. It would help the children as relating then could become unconditional in the family, person and behaviour could become separate and each person could be allowed to be their own individual self whilst respecting and valuing the individuality of the others.

Some children rebel against this narcissistic type of relating but in rebelling they take on the very characteristics of the parent against whom they are reacting. They will be rejected by this parent but will often get sneaking recognition and covert encouragement from the other passive parent. This then becomes a form of triangulation wherein the passive partner uses the child who rebels to get at the partner who dominates. The child, however, learns to use the same protective methods of narcissistic relating and in turn becomes just like the parent he is rebelling against.

Narcissistic relating is conditional loving and depending on its intensity and extremity it can lead to children becoming highly vulnerable to criticism and rejection. It certainly leads to poor self-esteem. The child continuously fears that he may not measure up to the unrealistic expectations of the parent who dominates. The conditions for gaining love and recognition may be:

- Be good for me
- Behave for me
- Do as you're told for me
- Be clever for me
- Be top of your class for me
- Be the helper for me
- Be like your brother or sister for me
- Be successful for me
- Be Catholic for me
- Be always there for me
- Be beautiful/handsome for me

Narcissistic relating may equally be expressed in terms of 'don'ts':

- Don't be yourself
- Don't contradict me
- Don't be different from me
- Don't think for yourself
- Don't be lazy
- Don't disobey
- Don't be irresponsible
- Don't be stupid
- Don't be low in your class
- Don't let me down in front of others
- Don't make your own decisions
- Don't lie to me
- Don't be separate from me
- Don't be ugly
- Don't talk
- Don't ask questions

It might seem from these lists that the narcissistic parent is totally selfish. Such a conclusion would be judgmental, critical and inaccurate and it would also confirm this parent's worst fear about herself. Recall that the preoccupation with 'me, me, me' arises from the subconscious fear of abandonment. It is the only way the person sees of ensuring that such rejection does not occur. It is not selfishness but a protection against rejection. The parent does not intentionally wish to harm or block her partner and children but, unwittingly, this is precisely what will happen.

Examples of narcissistic relating abound. They are most evident in the 'shoulds', 'should nots', 'have tos', 'musts' and 'ought tos' that are a common feature of most relationships:

- You should always be there for me
- You should not be late
- You should always be kind
- You should not disagree with me
- You should not have friends of your own

- Everything should be shared
- You should only love me
- You must do as I want
- You must not spend time away from me
- You must never be angry
- You must see things my way
- You ought to help me
- You ought never say 'no' to me

Checklist of problems of parents who narcissistically relate	
• Domineering behaviour	• Denial of vulnerability
• Controlling behaviour	• Dismissiveness
• Blaming behaviour	• Anxiety
• Rigidity	• Pushiness
• Criticism	• Arrogance
• Inflexibility	• Inability to listen
• Aggressiveness	• Live life through children
• Snobbishness	• Dependence
• Hypersensitivity	• Perfectionism
• Violence	

Because people who relate narcissistically do express their feelings, even if in an aggressive way, they are less prone to psychosomatic illness. However, they can sometimes neglect their physical welfare and their hidden worries and insecurities, along with long and intense working hours, can take a toll on their health. Psychosomatic conditions sometimes shown by such people include:

- Physical exhaustion
- Insomnia
- Arthritis
- Headaches
- Stomach ulcers
- Back pain
- Neck and shoulder tension
- Heart disease
- Cancer

The onset and duration of these conditions are related to the level of insecurity, the extent of the rigidity and hidden worrying, the severity of the perfectionism and the level of physical neglect of the parent who narcissistically relates to family members.

■ Overprotective caring

In many ways overprotective relating within families (and other social systems) is the opposite of narcissistic relating. Whereas the narcissistic parent is saying 'you are there for me', the overprotective parent is saying 'I am there for you'. Again, one of the parents usually sets the scene for this type of relating. Generally, it is the mother who tends to overprotect all the others within the family. Her partner lets her take all the responsibility as he does not feel secure enough to risk taking on responsibilities. Very often the man whose mother spoilt him will marry a woman who, in turn, will continue the process started in his childhood. Of course, this allows the woman to establish her identity through the caring behaviours. The dependence on being the helper reflects her self-esteem difficulties and any 'no' to her taking care of the man is responded to with withdrawal, sulking, accusations of 'you don't love me', crying, depression or intensification of efforts to do things for him. The hidden issue is 'I am terrified you will not need me as it is your dependence on me which ties you to me and without this bind you could not love me'. The aim of overprotective relating is to make yourself so indispensable that all others in the family cannot do without you. The result is that everyone in the family is disabled by being deprived of the opportunities to develop the capabilities of taking care of themselves emotionally, socially and domestically. The overprotective parent says: 'Once you allow me to take care of you, to wash you, cook for you, clean your room, choose your clothes, wash and iron your clothes, shop for you, be there when you come home, never be away from you, go everywhere with you, then I will love you and you will love me.'

Overprotective caring is just another type of conditional loving. It is a giving to get approval, recognition, love and acceptance. It is a martyrdom for the purpose of gaining visibility. The overprotective parent greatly neglects her own needs and gives priority always to others' needs. It is as if she were saying 'I don't count, you count'. Such people will sacrifice their own emotional, social, occupational, sexual, intellectual and creative development, seemingly for the sake of the other. If the person who narcissistically relates appears to take and take and take, the person who is overinvolved with others appears to give and give and give. Both, however, have a similar underlying problem of a sense of worthlessness; they are different from each other only in that they use different types of behaviour to try to reduce their feelings of insecurity.

The effects of overprotective relating on the self-esteem of other members of the family can be quite devastating. The parent who sets the overprotecting scene already has low self-esteem as has her partner. The children also develop self-esteem difficulties because subconsciously they realise that they are only loved conditionally through allowing this parent to live her life through them. The children in this situation develop no sense of capability and, as a result, seriously lack confidence. Even though the parent who overprotects will allow the children to have or do anything they wish, it must always happen through her. These children never learn to stand on their own two feet, to be independent, to develop a separate and unique identity; they have difficulty with new situations, may be overdemanding or underdemanding in relationships and have a deep lack of confidence. Ironically, overprotection can create narcissism and vice versa. Children either adapt to or rebel against the dominant type of relating in the family. When the child adapts, he becomes like the parent who overprotects and tends to be the 'people-pleaser' in and outside the home. When the child rebels, he goes the opposite way and becomes the 'taker' rather than the 'giver'. Either way the child will be low in self-esteem. It is very difficult for the child in the family that relates in an overbelonging way to separate out and become independent. Guilt feelings arise from the sense that the parent has done so much: how could one now go one's own way? In families that relate either narcissistically or overprotectively it is as if the umbilical cord had never really been cut and you never detach yourself to become your own individual, unique, independent and free self.

Checklist of problems of parents who overprotectively relate	
• Attention-seeking behaviour • Possessiveness • Clinging behaviour • Constantly seeking reassurance • Non-assertiveness • Passivity • Timidity • People-pleasing behaviour	• Neglect of self • Overactivity • Anxiety to please • Fear of not being good enough • Hypersensitivity to criticism • Difficulty in accepting help from others • Constantly complaining • Feelings easily hurt

Clearly the overprotective parent has a great need for acceptance and recognition, and dreads rejection. Some people have difficulty in understanding how the person who gives so much but frequently complains is actually looking for recognition. But the issue is quite clear: the complaining is an attempt to draw people's notice to all she has to do. Again it is a subconscious cry to be seen and valued. Similarly, the person who clings, who needs frequent reassurance, who people-pleases, who is tireless in helping others is also reaching out for visibility. However, there is the ever-underlying fear of rejection and abandonment by others. This unspoken fear, coupled with the neglect of one's physical, emotional, social and career needs and the tireless caring of others, can lead to the development of a range of psychosomatic conditions including:

- Heart disease
- Cancer
- Diabetes mellitus
- Arthritis
- Chrone's disease
- Panic attacks
- Phobias
- Tension headaches
- Back pain
- Ulcerative colitis

- Irritable bowel syndrome
- Multiple sclerosis
- Motor neuron disease
- Insomnia
- Hyperactivity
- Enduring fatigue

The onset and severity of these psychosomatic conditions are related to the depth of the insecurity of the person who is over-involved with others and to the extent of the neglect of self and the level of giving to others.

Regrettably, Western culture and religions have tended to reinforce the so-called selflessness of the parent, generally the mother, who sacrifices her life for the rest of the family. Her selflessness is seen as being loving and unselfish. But this is a myth that needs to be exposed. The 'selfless' parent is not at all unselfish, indeed quite the contrary. Her loving is a giving to get; it is conditional love which blocks not only her own development as a person but also the mature development of all other members of the family.

The children of the family where relating is overprotective may in their adulthood, in turn, develop psychological and psychosomatic problems similar to their parents. Some may develop psychological and social problems which are diametrically opposed to that of the parent who overprotects so that the child becomes overdemanding, insensitive to the needs of others and fearful of closeness. Such children, as adults, will tend to develop the psychological, social and psychosomatic problems that are more peculiar to the adult who relates narcissistically to others.

Children who adapt to the demands of overprotective relating will come into the school system already disabled in terms of their sense of their capabilities and will also doubt their lovability. Because they take on the behaviours of the parent who overprotects, they will want to please the teacher at all times and will be attention-seeking and hypersensitive to criticism. During the first days at school such children will have difficulty with this separation from the overinvolved parent. They may cry, get sick, be inconsolable and unresponsive to the caring of teachers. The separation may have to be done gently with the mother or father spending some time with the child until he is engrossed in some activity. The more dependent parent will probably take the child home, which is not a good idea. Some children will develop a school phobia but the problem is not in the school but within the home. At some subconscious level, the child recognises the vulnerability and dependence of the parent and is terrified of abandoning the person whom he relies on totally to meet all his needs. Separating out from this dependent parent is terrifying for the child as he fears both rejection and the possibility of no longer having needs met. When this child does get to school he is likely to be a model student but, of course, remains vulnerable to rejection by parents and teachers.

Children who rebel against overprotective behaviours in the family may dominate the parents through endless demands, temper tantrums and attempts at getting their own way at all times. It is important to remember that these children have self-esteem difficulties and are compensating for this through using aggressive, uncooperative, boastful and seemingly independent behaviours. They are trying to protect themselves against failure and the rejection which accompanies failure. At school these children may be inattentive in class, resistant to any correction, throw 'scenes' when the teacher attempts to be firm, hand up 'sloppy' homework or not do it at all. There is no firmness regarding responsibility in these children's homes because the parents fear that such demands might lead to their children not loving them. These children then learn to be irresponsible and all their needs continue to be met by their parents. Children always deserve to be loved but they need to learn that responsible behaviours earn reinforcements and irresponsible actions lead to loss of privileges. Such contingencies are essential for children to learn to be responsible within the home, school and elsewhere and their absence through overprotectiveness is detrimental to mature development.

❏ *The web of enmeshed family relationships*

A complex entangled web of interactions develops in enmeshed families. The parents' relationship with each other sets the scene for the way the whole family operates. The strength or weakness of the couple relationship largely determines how parents relate to their children. For example, the woman who feels neglected and dominated by her partner may attempt to meet her emotional needs through the children. The father may then resent the children whom he sees as coming between him and his partner. The children themselves will side either with the parent who narcissistically relates or with the parent who is passive in responding. Some children take on a protective role and rebel against the parent who is abusive of other family members. Children may attempt also to control or protect each other. In order to unravel this entanglement, the following relationships are considered separately below:

- parents' relationship with one another
- parents' relationships with the children
- children's relationships with the parents
- children's relationships with one another.

■ Parents' relationship with one another
It has been pointed out already that opposites attract each other in terms of the protective behaviours each employs against hurt and rejection. In enmeshed couple relationships a man who, for example, protects himself through narcissism will be attached to a woman who people-pleases in order to gain acceptance. In this relationship both their protective patterns will be reinforced by his dominating and controlling and by her passivity and eagerness to please. The continuation of these protective patterns serves to maintain each partner's vulnerability. Unless these patterns of behaviour are confronted and changed, their protective power weakens over time and the partners become more threatened by the way they are relating to each other.

Take the example of the man who regularly dominates, controls and criticises his wife. She, for her part, is operating passively like one of her own parents who, in their turn, were responsible for her present negative feelings about herself. As a result of repeated experiences of rejection and of never feeling good enough, the wife may either increase her passivity and her attempts to please her husband or begin to hide behind masks of anxiety or depression or completely withdraw from her husband. Furthermore, she may now shift her dependent need for love to the children and this in turn will begin to threaten their self-image. When the wife who is passive begins to retreat from her husband, he becomes more threatened and will either escalate his protective dominant behaviours or begin to stay out of home more and more.

A similar process takes place in the case of the wife who relates narcissistically to a husband who is quiet and passive. With endless demands, criticism and sarcasm, his protection of giving in and pleasing her may no longer stem her tide of rejecting behaviours and he is then compelled subconsciously to invent other protective behaviours. Patterns of silence and withdrawal and 'just letting her do what she wants' are very likely here. However, he may now begin to form a dependent relationship with one of the children and may even covertly urge the child to rebel against his dominating partner. The web now becomes more and more enmeshed.

I recall one family with whom I worked where the wife screeched and screamed her way through the years of the marriage, and the husband, who had a dread of conflict, gave in constantly to her ever-increasing, unreasonable demands. After fifteen years of this ongoing abusive behaviour, he developed an extramarital relationship, which was eventually discovered. My point to both of them was that the extramarital relationship was but a symptom of the very unsatisfactory and immature relationship which had existed between them. Unless she ceased her dominating and controlling behaviour and he desisted from giving in to her, there was no hope of progress in their relationship. The man's wife was targeting the 'other woman' as the cause of the problems, thereby avoiding responsibility for her own part in her problematic marital relationship. Of course, the husband, by having an extramarital affair, was also avoiding his responsibility for his passivity in his marriage relationship and his responsibility for ensuring his right to a respecting, valuing and equal relationship. The children had also been deeply affected by their parents' troubled relationship. Both parents had themselves come from troubled homes:

he had been totally dominated by a father who was rigid and overbearing; her mother had totally dominated her father and she, in identifying with her mother, had developed similar characteristics and had, unwittingly, repeated her parents' marital relationship in her own marriage.

■ Parents' relationships with the children

You have seen that when parents do not have a positive couple relationship, a coalition may be formed between a parent and a child. In this case the parent may attempt to meet in the relationship with the child, the emotional, social and sometimes sexual needs not being met in the couple relationship. I remember working with one couple who had one son aged ten years. Their couple relationship had become strained very early on and the mother had become overinvolved with her son, taking him to her bed which he was still occupying at ten years of age. The boy's father hated him as he saw him as the one who came between him and his partner. The more hostility the father showed to the child, the more the mother pushed him away and drew the child closer to her. The child had become the means for both of them to avoid looking at the deeper issues of their own poor self-esteem, their dependence on each other and their very problematic relationship. The overprotective behaviour of the mother and the neglectful behaviour of the father towards their son were having deep psychological, social and physical effects on the child. The boy was asthmatic, fearful and timid; he felt unloved by his father and smothered by his mother. He missed many school days and was very poor at mixing with his peers.

Many parents live their lives through their children. They want their children to be clever, beautiful and successful so that they can feel good as parents. Quite innocently, these parents boast of their children's achievements. These parents are revealing their own poor sense of self, their dependence on the opinions and acceptance of others and their possessiveness of their children's lives.

I have come across many parents who, because of their own insecurity, dominate and control at least one member of the family to ensure that he is always there for the parent. Rarely does this child as an adult leave the home or get married. He will have been deeply conditioned to believe that it is his role to look after the parents (even though they may be quite active and healthy). Any attempt to separate out from this enmeshment is likely to be met by guilt-inducing statements such as:

- 'How will we ever manage without you?'
- 'Your place is here with us'
- 'Is it that you don't love us any more?'
- 'What do you mean you're entitled to live your own life, what kind of crap is that?'

There are so many ways that parents' relationships with their children can block their mature development. Clearly, an incestuous relationship between father and daughter or between mother and son can have devastating effects. I have helped many women who experienced sexual abuse at the hands of their father and the effects on their whole development were deeply damaging. Their physical self-esteem was extremely poor, their sense of being lovable was totally absent, they found forming relationships with others very difficult and their outlook on life was dismal. It is good that in the last decade women have started to speak out about their childhood sexual abuse experiences. My own belief is that there is also a hidden well of abuse experiences among men that has yet to be revealed.

Parents who are regularly irritable, dismissive, impatient, dogmatic, rigid, scolding, ridiculing, sarcastic or cynical in their interactions with their children have long-term negative effects on the development of their children's self-esteem. But it must be remembered that when parents relate in such ways with children this happens because of their own self-esteem difficulties, their problematic couple relationship and, very often, the frustrations, hurts, feelings of failure and feelings of 'not being good enough' that they bring home from their places of work. The more enmeshed parents are in their interactions with children – whether through dominance, aggression or over-protection – the more difficult life will be for those children.

- Children's relationships with the parents

I have come across families where the children dominate the
parents. These children have been given inordinate power in the
household and can hold the parents to ransom by, for example,
threatening to leave, to hurt themselves or to kill themselves.
The parents in such families lack parenting skills but also may
feel quite powerless as individuals to counter the behaviours
of the children. The children may miss school whenever they
feel like it, and rage when any attempt is made to ensure responsible behaviour.

In other homes a child may 'parent' the parents by becoming the 'carer' within the family. Such a child takes care of a
parent who seems helpless and may also attempt to offset negative reactions of the other parent by being always one step
ahead in meeting his needs. This child may go to untold lengths
to have the house clean, meals ready, fire lit, newspaper in,
garden weeded and so on. The child may, in very adult ways,
nurture, soothe, encourage, praise and be affectionate towards
both parents. The problem is, of course, that the child is not
an adult and this unfair burden of parenting means that the
child misses out on many important developmental milestones.
This child as an adult will find it difficult to separate out from
the 'parenting' role developed at a young age.

In other troubled families the child may become the 'go-
between' or the 'peacemaker'. Any hint of possible conflict
between the parents and this child will find some way of
distracting them from the conflictual issue. The child may 'act
up', may get sick, may attempt to draw one of the parents into
an activity or may get upset. These are all ploys to stop the
conflict because the child's world is seriously threatened by
parental rows. When the child fails in his attempts to stop the
conflict there is a danger that he may develop a serious illness
in order to stop parents fighting. I remember one six-year-old
child who had developed serious cancer and was not responsive
to treatment. Her parents were in continual violent conflict
and she had done all in her power to go between them and stop
their hurting of each other and their neglect of her. Sadly, she
constantly failed. However, when she developed cancer both

parents switched their attention to her – she had finally won! The danger was that the 'victory' would cost her her life. The parents came for individual and marital therapy (thereby taking the responsibility off the child's shoulders) and as their relationship began to improve, the child began also to show signs of recovery.

Sometimes when parents are in conflict a child will side with one of the parents in order to protect that parent. There is a subconscious wisdom to this: 'If one parent can be kept healthy and loving of me then I create some security for myself.' Some children who exhibit school phobias are staying home to look after a vulnerable parent with whom they have a good relationship. Generally these children do not have a good relationship with the other parent.

When a parent is overdemanding and critical, the children may avoid contact with that parent and 'be gone' from the home most of the time. Where the other parent is passive and overprotective these children will attempt to get all their needs met through that parent. They will rarely approach the parent who relates narcissistically for fulfilment of their needs. The common response of the overloaded parent in this family is 'why don't you ask your father (or mother)?', a comment likely to be met by 'he wouldn't give it' or 'I'd be wasting my time' or 'you know the answer will be no, no, no'.

In yet other enmeshed families a child may rebel against the dominating, critical parent and become the aggressive protector of other members' rights within the family. These children will now have a very difficult relationship with the targeted parent and, without realising it, will use the same faulty methods of relating that are the object of the rebellious behaviours. Here, aggression breeds aggression, hostility breeds hostility and in spite of the well-intentioned attempts of the child, family disharmony continues to escalate.

■ Children's relationships with one another

An underestimated influence in enmeshed families is how siblings relate to each other. I know of a family where one brother had a very difficult childhood because of an older brother's aggression towards him. This aggression was a displace-ment by the older brother of feelings of anger towards his parents onto his younger brother, since to show hostility to parents would mean risking further hurt. Because the relation-ship with a brother or sister is not as important as the need for acceptance by parents, children are prepared to risk the relation-ship with each other in order to gain acceptance from parents.

Competition between children – revealed in name-calling and competing with each other in games, school achievements, looks, household tasks and so on – affects the self-esteem of the oppos-ing parties. Being better than one's brother or sister is an attempt to gain recognition from parents: 'Look what a wonderful child I am and how bad by comparison my brother is.'

It is well known that a child may be upset by the arrival of a new baby. Very often the older children revert to babyish behaviour themselves. They are terrified of not getting their needs met and their protestations are an attempt to bring their insecurities to their parents' attention. When parents respond in an understanding and loving way to their fears, children adjust to the presence of the newcomer. However, if parents become irritable and critical then these children's worst fears are being realised. They may now either escalate their over-demanding behaviour or begin to withdraw in order to protect themselves from any further hurt or rejection. Either way, they lose out. In situations where the neglect is great there is a danger that the baby may be at risk from an older child, if he is deeply troubled. It would not be wise to leave this child alone with the baby as he may take his anger out on the baby. When these issues are not resolved, this sibling rivalry can persist into old age.

Very often older children are allowed to dominate younger children because parents feel unable to correct such damaging relationships between their children. The effect can be a lot of misery for the dominated child. It can also mean that children who are dominating and aggressive set themselves up for much condemnation by parents. When this happens the younger child may constantly needle the older sibling into being aggressive – 'Mum, John is at me again' – resulting in the mother scolding the older boy and embracing the younger child.

Other children try to please their brothers and sisters both to protect themselves from parental scolding and also to get acceptance from siblings. Some children protect one another from the wrath of parents by covering up for each other. This relationship can lead to strong protective bonds which persist into adulthood and may lead to an overdependence on each other. Whilst in childhood the protection was a necessary strategy for the children, in adulthood it may hinder the development of independence and an ability to stand on one's own two feet.

❏ *Changing enmeshed family relationships*

Family problems are best seen as challenges that all family members can take on in order to create a more harmonious family. What counts is effort; the more persistent and consistent the effort the better. Along the road of change old patterns of neglect are likely to be repeated; this must not become the reason for quitting or criticising or condemning yourself. Such failures need to be seen as opportunities for further learning and effort. When family members apologise for and talk out experiences of neglect, then the rift in the relationship can be quickly healed.

In order to overcome any problem it is essential to get to the cause. When you know the cause you have the 'cure'. Recall the two types of enmeshed family relationships: narcissistic and overprotective. Typical behaviours of the narcissistic parent include dominating, controlling, blaming, criticising, ridiculing, irritability, physical punishment and dismissal of others' needs. Typical behaviours of the overprotective parent include timidity, manipulation, possessiveness, non-assertiveness, neglect of self, people-pleasing and constant seeking of reassurance. But the causes of both types of relating lie primarily in the parent's family of origin: very often that family's problematic relationship pattern is being repeated in the new family. The alternative ways of relating that will undo the past and create a happier and more mature present are:

- Creating unconditional loving relationships (Chapter 4)
- Meeting the reasonable needs of each member of the family (Chapter 6)

- Valuing and maturely expressing feelings within the family (Chapter 7)
- Developing caring and effective means of communication between family members (Chapter 8)
- Fairly allocating responsibilities within the family (Chapter 9)
- Managing and controlling behaviour that leads to neglect of responsibilities within the family (Chapter 9)
- Creating a family environment wherein each member's self-esteem is continuously enhanced (Chapter 10)
- Developing the independence of each member of the family so that emotional leavetaking is possible (Chapter 11)

Chapter 5 looks in detail at the systematic steps to be taken in resolving family disharmony. However, it is the everyday efforts to create family interactions along the lines just outlined that provide the healing and mature ground for change. The process is the same for both the parent who relates narcissistically and the parent who relates overprotectively, except that each has to let go of a different set of fears and protective behaviours. It is important that the narcissistic parent does not blame himself but sees such maladaptive behaviours as a revelation and an opportunity to change matters within self and between self and others. The overprotective parent needs to realise that overprotective caring does not benefit anyone in the family. Because it is generally the case that the person who is narcissistic marries a person who overprotects and relates passively, both parents need to develop awareness of their own individual protective behaviours and to take on the responsibility of creating a family environment wherein each is unconditionally valued, respected, loved and encouraged towards responsibility and independence.

Clearly the process is complex and multifaceted, and parents – the family architects – need knowledge, the support of each other and the support of other parents to pursue the task of creating a happy family. If either or both parents have difficulty in following through the recommendations made in this book and find themselves resorting regularly to enmeshed relating, it would be wise to seek outside assistance such as a training group for parents, a family therapist or a clinical psychologist, psychotherapist, psychoanalyst or counsellor well versed in family dynamics.

CHAPTER 3

Changing the Neglectful Family

- ❏ *'No win' neglectful family relationships*
  - Absence of care
  - Loveless caring
  - Symbiotic caring
- ❏ *The web of neglectful family relationships*
  - Parents' relationship with one another
  - Parents' relationships with the children
  - Children's relationships with the parents
  - Children's relationships with one another
- ❏ *Changing neglectful family relationships*

Character builds slowly but it can be torn down
with incredible swiftness.
Faith Baldwin

❏ *'No win' neglectful family relationships*

Fortunately, 'no win' neglectful family relationships are less frequent than 'win at a cost' enmeshed family relationships. In 'no win' families the members have no way of gaining love, recognition and independence. It is a stalemate situation whose effects on all family members' self-esteem and on the relationships between them are extremely serious. The members of this kind of family seldom emerge from the scars of the gross emotional neglect they suffer without going for professional help. These grossly neglectful family relationships can be categorised under three headings:

- absence of care
- loveless caring
- symbiotic caring.

■ Absence of care

The relationship characterised by an absence of care is an extremely damaging relationship. These relationships were common in orphanages where no one adult established any close contact with the orphan child; indeed establishing such a relationship was very much frowned upon. I have worked with many people who have had an early history of neglect and, without exception, their self-esteem was rock bottom. These people saw themselves as being invisible and as not being deserving of any love, affection, warmth or kindness. When there is an absence of care in a family, it is a 'no win' situation for all its members because no matter what they do – be it good, bad or indifferent – no recognition, acceptance or love will be gained.

I remember once, having given a talk on parenting, being approached by a couple in their mid-thirties who expressed a lot of concern over their relationship with their recently adopted son, who was seven years of age. They complained that they had showered the boy with love and kindness over the past three months but no positive response was forthcoming. They admitted to genuinely thinking of not going through with the adoption. On enquiring about the child's past I was told that he had been in twenty different foster homes up to the time of his adoption. Because of this history of rejection experiences this child had learned not to trust affection as it could be so suddenly taken away. It was safer for him to retire into his own world and not respond. I advised the adoptive parents to persevere in showing the child love. I also pointed out to them that love is best given freely and unconditionally, and that to give love in order to get love back was unlikely to succeed with this child. He needed to learn that whether or not he responded, love was present every day for him. His adoptive parents agreed to follow my suggestion. About a year later, when I met them accidentally, the mother rushed over to tell me that only two weeks previously the child had spontaneously hugged her and that he was beginning to respond to their warmth towards him. The breakthrough had come and now I was optimistic that the emotional scars this child had suffered would finally begin to heal.

One of the sad aspects of early experiences of neglect is that they tend to be unwittingly perpetuated in later years. The 'no win' situation can then lead to a hopelessness, a belief that no action will ever gain recognition, acceptance and affection. I recall one male client describing his experience of being reared in such a family as 'I always felt invisible'. His invisibility had continued into adulthood. As a married man his wife totally dominated him. In his job, even though he was a supervisor, he never said 'no' to requests of him and placed everybody else's needs before his own. That man's invisibility, and of others like him, is illustrated in the following poem I wrote in response to the sad news of his suicide.

Invisible Man

It took an
invisible man
to get me
to see
what it means
not to be seen

To his wife
he was low life
to be led
and said
by her needs,
his not to heed

In corners
he hid from others.
Pass me by
his cry.
His presence
had no essence

At school age
pent-up rage,
much got at
named rat
he hurried,
from jibes scurried.

In mates' eyes
second rate.
To feel good
they could
joke and cut
into his gut.

In his home
parents numb
to love needs.
Indeed
a swelled head
he never had

Not in vain
did he not refrain
from laying . . .
staying . . .
for the train
to end his pain.

There are those
I care for and lose
with sadness . . .
helpless . . .
to me still
full visible

Parents who grossly neglect their children tend also to be totally neglectful of their own welfare. More rarely, it is because the parents are so caught up in their own lives that they forget their children also have needs. Whatever the causes, the absence of relating leads to the development of very low self-esteem in children and the further exacerbation of the parents' own poor self-esteem. Sadly, the children turn out like the parents, unable to form relationships. These parents then feel rejected by their children, not realising that children need to experience love in order to be able to give it to others.

In some families not only is there an absence of positive relating, but there is the presence of active emotional, physical and sexual abuse. Many women clients have told me of how they were regularly sexually abused by their fathers from an early age. In some cases mothers colluded with such abuse. Not to be loved by one parent is a tragedy, not to be cherished by either is devastating and deeply affects people for the rest of their lives unless some professional help is found to undo the history of rejection.

Parents in this type of family can manifest a variety of seriously disturbing problems:

- Extremely poor self-esteem
- Depression
- Manic depression
- Paranoia
- Extreme egotism
- Delusions
- Hallucinations
- Alcohol dependence
- Drug dependence
- Lack of emotion
- Extreme compulsive and/or obsessional behaviours
- Violence
- Sexually abusive behaviour
- Sexual deviance
- Withdrawal from all social contact
- Suicide attempts

Regrettably, when parents manifest any of these problems, the children tend to develop either similar problems or diametrically opposed behaviours. An example of the latter reaction is where a child of alcoholic parents develops an extreme aversion to taking any kind of alcoholic drink. A further example is the young woman who was sexually abused as a child and who becomes totally asexual as an adult. The problem in such cases is that the opposite type of behaviour developed is as extreme as the behaviour against which the person is reacting, and these protective reactions are brought into the relationships the person forms in adulthood. For example, the fanaticism over alcohol or the total lack of interest in sex will create problems in the couple relationship and later on within the newly formed family. I recall one woman whose parents were both alcohol dependent and had grossly neglected and physically abused her. When her four children came into their teenage years, she continually preached about the evils of alcohol and used to constantly check on them, smell their breath, question their whereabouts and so on. Each one of them became alcohol dependent. The very thing this woman dreaded she unwittingly brought about by her own extreme behaviours.

The lack of relating or the presence of gross emotional, physical or sexual abuse leaves the children of such a family bereft of any sense of value in themselves. They often feel they are ugly, despicable, a nuisance, worthless and only deserving of pain and rejection. These children rarely thrive academically. Emotionally they are too traumatised to be able to cognitively apply themselves within a classroom. Unaware, they adopt ways that perpetuate the pain of their childhood by setting themselves up for ridicule, scoldings, criticism and rejection.

▪ Loveless caring

Within the loveless family there may be a lot of material and instrumental caring but there are no expressions of love; no warmth, support, nurturance, active listening, compassion, understanding or empathy. It resembles in many ways the family where there is an absence of relating, as in both there is total neglect of the members' emotional well-being and there is no way for anyone in the family to gain love and a feeling of being valued. Very often, work and ambition dominate this family. The parents subconsciously use work as a means of protecting themselves against any emotional closeness. Such closeness would threaten self-esteem as neither parent feels lovable and to risk showing affection or receiving affection would mean risking rejection.

Neither can the parents reach out in love to their children, as again, subconsciously, they are convinced that their children would reject them. It is safer for them to focus on providing for material well-being. Very often, when they bring a troubled child for help they say quite innocently: 'We've given her everything and we can't imagine why she should be insecure or unhappy.' They may very well have provided for her in terms of a home, education, luxury items, clothes, recreation facilities, pocket money and so on, but the real question is whether they have given her of their time, whether they have regularly shown affection and warmth, whether they have held the girl and expressed love, whether they have listened and responded to her fears, anxieties, doubts about herself, worries about the future. Inevitably, the response to such questions is one of silence. At one level the parents know that their child needs emotional caring, but at a deeper subconscious level they do not know how to show such caring nor could they show it even if they knew how, as the risk of experiencing a repeat of the rejection they themselves experienced as children is too great.

A young man of twenty years of age was referred to me by the family doctor because he had become very withdrawn, was failing to attend lectures in his third-level college and was socially isolated. He was living away from home. There were indications he was delusional. There was also neglect of his physical well-being and he was very much underweight. This young man believed that everybody in Ireland knew about him, that he was the object of a special study. He believed he was particularly known by the best-known television and radio presenters. He also brought me a huge amount of notebooks, all written up in a very tight script. These notebooks contained various fantasy stories all depicting himself as the central character. When I spoke with his parents, his mother quite innocently said: 'You know doctor, I never gave him any affection or praise because it might have given him a swelled head.' A swelled head indeed he had, but swelled with fantasies crying out to be seen, recognised and loved – all the things she had failed to give him. His father was a very quiet, reserved and silent man who in a different way also failed to give the boy what he needed. How wise of the boy's psyche to compensate in his fantasy world for what was not present in reality. I explained the boy's problem to his parents and recommended that the three of them come into therapy together – after all the parents needed as much healing as the boy. Both parents had very low self-esteem, were in a loveless marriage and, unfortunately, had created a loveless family. Within three months of family therapy all the delusions and fantasy writings had ceased. Therapy mainly focused on getting each of them to show love for each other in a myriad of ways on a daily basis. Further progress occurred over the following year, and over time the changes achieved were not only maintained but also considerably deepened.

When a child in an emotionless family reaches out naturally for love and affection she will not get a response and may even be dismissed in a harsh way. A common protective weapon used by the parents in this kind of family is silence. When a child crosses the line into some 'no go' emotional area – such as the expression of affection, anger, sadness or upset – the parent will often not talk to the child for a period of time and may seek the cooperation of other members of the family in not talking to this 'bold' child. Children quickly learn what pleases and what displeases parents, and in such a family they will learn to suppress all feelings and become in turn like their emotionless parents.

The parents of the family characterised by loveless caring may display any of the following problems:

• Very low self-esteem	• Compulsive behaviour
• Lack of emotion	• Withdrawal
• Workaholism	• Rigid attitudes
• Perfectionism	• Authoritarianism
• Obsessional behaviour	• Sexual impotency/frigidity

The parents, and subsequently the children, of the loveless family tend to develop a whole range of psychosomatic problems including:

• Asthma	• Arthritis
• Cancer	• Irritable bowel syndrome
• Abdominal pain	• Ulcerative colitis
• Heart disease	• Migraine
• Hypertension	

It is important to realise that the parents in these troubled families have an enormous need to be loved and valued but are terrified of reaching out. They tend to be very hard on themselves (and on others), driving themselves and putting unrealistic work demands on themselves. It is the cutting off of their feelings and the immense physical pressure they put on themselves that eventually lead to psychosomatic conditions.

I remember a man in his mid-twenties who was in the advanced stages of cancer of the lower abdomen and had been given a short time to live by medical consultants. During the initial interview, he related to me the number of operations he had had and the frightful side-effects of the radium therapy; that he was a young professional man engaged to be married; and that the medical consultant reckoned he had about six months to live. During his telling of all these traumatic experiences what stood out most clearly was the absence of any emotion, be it sadness, fear, anger or rage. Indeed, a fixed smile remained on his face during the entire time. Medical research shows that people who mask their true feelings with a more or less permanently smiling countenance are very prone to cancer. Coupled with this masking is the inability to express feelings due to fear of rejection. I attempted to help this young man to see how he was repressing hostile feelings but he had huge difficulty in making this connection. However, at the very end of the interview he said: 'You know Tony, I know I have some awful feeling stuck down in the pit of my stomach for years.' What subsequently transpired was that he felt his mother never loved him and the 'awful' feeling was one of rejection counterpointed by a tremendous need to be loved. He had been reared in a loveless home and any show of feeling was dismissed, ignored, laughed at, or punished. Once, in a visualisation exercise I did with him, much to his surprise he found a small smooth stone in an old chest. He could not understand the significance of this until we traced it back to a time in his childhood when, in times of emptiness and loneliness, he used to go to a local beach and find smooth stones that he loved to touch. It was a compensatory way of getting the holding he was not getting at home. I was deeply moved by this young man's story and wrote the following poem for him:

Touchstone

On empty beach
waves touch
the tide of woe
in you did sow
a dark foe

In loveless home
face numbs
when feelings lone
cut to the bone
no touchstone

I picked alone
smooth stones
as you did then
to ease your pain
deep within

The emotional starvation which I believe led to his cancer strongly emerged when he said to me: 'Why is it that I had to get cancer for my mother to tell me for the first time that she loved me?' The answer was that a human being will go to any lengths to find the love that he deeply needs. The cancer had got him what he most wanted. He died nine months later, having learned to express much love to his fiancée, parents, friends and, most of all, to himself. He told me that even though he knew he was dying, the discoveries and the love experience of his last nine months had brought him a happiness and fulfilment he had never known before.

A family where there is relating without feeling is a highly disturbing place to be. The parents have no sense of their lovability and capability. They strive to avoid repeating the pain of rejection experienced in their own childhood by being intensely involved in some non-threatening activity – usually work. The children of this family emerge with low self-esteem, with an inability to express or receive feelings, and with protective ways to avoid rejection – such as the belief that work is the be all and end all of life. These children very often thrive academically because of their dedication to instrumental activities.

However, behind the facade, they are deeply distressed and do not attain happiness, contentment or fulfilment through their academic success. Regrettably, they are likely, as adults, to develop the psychological problems of their parents. Research has clearly shown that the life expectancy of people reared in families where care is either absent or loveless is greatly reduced compared with that of persons from families where love and caring are the dominant features.

■ Symbiotic caring

Within the symbiotic family everyone must be the same and have the same ideas on everything: no difference or individuality is allowed. It is as if the family is the individual and each member is but a part. Monasteries and convents are often symbiotic places. I spent several years in a monastery where we dressed the same, walked the same way, ate the same food, went to bed at the same time, had to have the same ideas, had to watch the same TV programmes and had to take part in games whether we liked it or not. I remember that during the latter years of my stay I began to question many of the rules, regulations, beliefs, attitudes and culture of monastic life. I was struggling within myself as I had begun to lose all belief in religious systems. My queries, and sometimes anger, were genuine expressions of my own inner turmoil. None of these individual needs of mine was taken into account. It seemed that I was a threat to the fabric of the system. Various attempts were made to get me to conform including threats, exclusion and being prevented from going forward for ordination with my classmates. The last straw was when it was suggested I be sent to a priest psychologist to sort out my differences. In a healthy system differences are valued and appreciated but in a symbiotic system they are highly threatening and have to be suppressed.

The symbiotic family is completely insular and attempts to meet all needs within the family. Outsiders are excluded and children, for example, are rarely allowed bring friends home. The parents themselves most likely have come from symbiotic families. They would probably have lived at home up to the time of their marriage. Very often the offspring of this family never marry.

I remember one young woman, recently married, who was already having marital problems. She had come from a symbiotic family and was living a few doors down the terrace from her home of origin. I happened to visit both homes and was struck by the sameness between them. I reckoned this woman had not left home at all and was attempting to re-create her home of origin. Neither had her parents let go of her and they were heavily involved in her life. Curiously, with unconscious wisdom, she had married a man who always wanted to be out. He too had come from an insecure home and had learned to protect himself from hurt and rejection by absenting himself. She had learned the opposite: she got her needs met by always being in the home. Symbiotic relating means that the members of the family are so dependent on one another that they cannot live without each other. An attempt on the part of any member to separate, be independent or be just plain different will cause this family to break down. In this young woman's marriage she felt threatened and neglected because her husband always wanted to be out and he, in turn, felt suffocated, fearful and rejected because she always wanted him to be in. Both had very deep self-esteem problems and only when these were being addressed were they able to work on the couple relationship. She gradually learned that his wanting to be out was not a message about her worth and he learned a similar lesson with regard to her wanting him to be in. She needed to learn some of his 'being out' behaviour and he needed to learn some of her 'being in' behaviour. Both were extreme in their behaviour to begin with but eventually a middle ground was found. This could not have happened while their self-esteem was low as any demand for change would then be experienced as a threat to their sense of themselves.

Like neglectful or emotionless families, the symbiotic family is destructive of the healthy development of each of its members. There is no celebration, no encouragement of uniqueness and difference. The system is far more important than the individual needs of any one member. The members of this family subconsciously believe that each cannot do without the others and that the sameness that binds them together is what will save them. But the human psyche has a need to be individual. When the blocks to that development are monumental then it takes 'block-busting' actions to gain recognition. It is no accident that schizophrenia occurs more often in symbiotic than in other types of families. It is the psyche attempting to express individuality and, most of all, to gain love. Typically, people who have been labelled schizophrenic suffer from paranoia, delusions and hallucinations. The person who is paranoid believes that everybody knows about him, that he is special, and that things happen that demonstrate his specialness. In reality this person is not seen and the paranoid behaviour so aptly expresses the need of this person who has been so badly neglected and hurt in life.

Delusional behaviour has the same function. I have helped individuals who were convinced they were Jesus Christ or the devil. It is interesting that the delusion always involves somebody well known within the person's culture. I have never come across a person in Ireland or England who believed he was the Buddha. I remember one young man who claimed he was Jesus Christ. After announcing this to me, he said 'are you going to lock me up now?', and I said 'why would I do that?' It transpired he had been in and out of mental hospitals for the last nine years of his life. He then said to me 'but do you believe I'm Jesus Christ?' I replied that I was sure there were very good reasons why he needed to be Jesus Christ. It eventually emerged that up to the time of his first delusional experience he was never seen for himself within his family. But the Jesus Christ delusion got him a lot of recognition. It was curious that he knew this at some level because when I asked him 'what do you gain from being Jesus Christ?', he quickly answered 'recognition'. I then asked him what did he gain from being James Green (fictitious name) and the answer came quickly and unhesitatingly, 'anonymity'. The process of therapy was clear. I had to help this man to feel loved, seen, valued and celebrated for himself. He himself was the person who most needed to see him in this way. In a similar way, hallucinations express the inner, unmet needs of the individual whose self-esteem is extremely low.

When children from a symbiotic family come to school, they will be very conformist and generally will work hard. However, emotionally and socially these children do not integrate. They will be quiet, passive, shy, timid and withdrawn but will not present any problems in the classroom. It is in adolescence that the attempt to break through to the wider world occurs, and when it does it often takes a seemingly bizarre form. The adolescent in this case is not only trying to save herself from anonymity but is also attempting to save the rest of the family. Unfortunately, the rest of the family are likely to respond in a very rejecting way to the adolescent who shows schizophrenic-type behaviours. They will be 'happy' to see her locked away so that they can go back to their cocoon of sameness again. Her difference threatens that sameness, and the more extreme the difference the greater the threat. The whole family needs therapy. Separating the adolescent in question by means of individual therapy may in the long term benefit her, but the family will not have changed and her return to that family will put her at risk again.

❏ *The web of neglectful family relationships*

As for the enmeshed family, a web of neglectful relationships develops within 'no win' families. Again, how the parents relate (or fail to relate) to each other will determine largely the way they relate to the children and in turn how the children relate to them and to each other. Generally speaking, parents who are neglectful of each other's welfare also neglect their children. When parents do not show any caring for each other or are violent towards each other, children often repeat these patterns towards the parents and towards each other. Sometimes, the children rebel and do exactly the opposite of the parents. Either way, neglectful patterns continue. In order to give some further insight into the web of neglectful family relationships these relationships are considered separately below under the headings of:

- parents' relationship with one another
- parents' relationships with the children
- children's relationships with the parents
- children's relationships with one another.

■ Parents' relationship with one another

The couple relationship within the highly neglectful family is
one where there may be:

- Frequent open conflict of both a verbal and physical nature
- Possessiveness and overinvolvement with each other that
  excludes other relationships (even with children)
- An overinvolvement of both parents with the family that
  excludes any expression of independence and individuality
  on their part or on the children's part
- An overemphasis on career development, money and material
  possessions but no expression of feelings
- Frequent abuse of alcohol, neglect of physical and emotional
  well-being, and dependence on prescribed or illegal drugs

It is clear that in couple relationships with these characteristics
neither the self-esteem of either partner nor the relationship
between them will flourish. Too often the pattern of behaviour
manifested is a repeat of that experienced in the couple's
families of origin. Their children in turn, in witnessing such
a neglectful relationship between their parents, are likely to
repeat it in their adult lives as they will not have experienced
many other couple relationships in their formative years. From
an early age children of these parents start to engage in neglect
of themselves and other family members. Sometimes, children
will behave in exactly the opposite way to the parents who are
neglectful but this, in turn, though not as damaging, can create
other problems.

As in other relationships, opposites also attract in neglectful couples. For example, you may find a woman from a symbiotic family (the family whose members are always in) being
attracted to a man from a family where no caring was shown
(the family whose members are always out). This relationship is likely to deteriorate quickly because he will interpret
her 'always needing to be in and not going out with him' as
rejection and she will interpret his 'always being out and not
wanting to stay in with her' as rejection. Initially each will
escalate the pressure: pressure by her on him to stay in and

pressure by him on her to come out. When this pressure does not produce the desired effects, either aggression or withdrawal occurs. Likewise you may find an individual coming from a loveless home, where emphasis was put on work and material possessions, marrying somebody who tends to be totally irresponsible in these particular areas. Criticism of each other is likely to quickly emerge leading to feelings of rejection and the onset of open conflict or withdrawal. Another typical match is the violent man and the extremely passive woman. His violence is seen as rejection by her and her withdrawal is seen as rejection by him. These experiences of feeling rejected will quickly spiral leading to the occurrence of emotional, physical or sexual abuse between them.

■ Parents' relationships with the children

Parents of families where 'no win' relationships predominate may be neglectful of themselves in any of the following ways:

- Neglectful of physical welfare (drug abuse, poor diet, alcohol abuse, overweight, underweight, heavy smoking)
- Neglectful of emotional and social welfare (isolated, withdrawn, abusive, violent, loud, argumentative, rigid, obsessional, compulsive, hallucinatory, delusional)
- Neglectful of development of responsible behaviours ('dropping out', voluntary unemployment, unhygienic home, lack of basic physical resources, lack of self-control)

Generally, parents will relate to their children the way they relate to themselves. Children in 'no win' family relationships are frequently the victims of a whole range of abuses. For example, their educational development either may be not catered for at all or may be overemphasised at the expense of other more urgent needs. Parents in such families often expect too much from their children, wanting them, for example, to take care of themselves before they can barely walk. The children may be loaded with many of the responsibilities that the parents are not carrying. Physical and sexual abuse are not uncommon in 'no win' families.

■ Children's relationships with the parents

What a sad plight the children of neglectful parents are in:
they need so much to be loved but have no hope of getting it.
These children are likely to develop the protective behaviours
described below in their relationships with their parents in
order to reduce the possibilities of further hurt.

Protective behaviour	Message to parents
Avoidance of contact (being out of home as much as possible)	'I can't be hurt when I'm not around you.'
Extreme parent-pleasing	'If I do everything right will you stop rejecting and hurting me?'
Aggression (fighting fire with fire)	'If I become like you, maybe you will accept me.'
Living in a fantasy world	'I can only find some happiness by not living in the real world with you.'
Hallucinations and delusions (for example, taking on the identity of well-known figures or believing everybody in the world knows about you)	'Will you accept me when I am not myself?' or 'I have to act insane before I get any recognition from you.'
Dependence on drugs, alcohol or glue sniffing	'When I put myself out of this world I dull the pain of your rejection of me.'
Illness	'If I'm sick will you stop rejecting me?'
Apathy	'If I do nothing then I can't get it wrong' or 'It is too risky to do anything in this family.' →

| Unacceptable social behaviour (for example, violence, robbery, sexual and physical abuse of others) | 'Do you see what you have driven me to do?' or 'The only way I get recognition in this world is by abusing others; this is what you have taught me.' |

I have worked with children, adolescents and adults who have enacted these protective behaviours in their relationships with parents. However, these protective behaviours only partially work and their attempts are frustrated by their contempt for themselves, by their parents' inability to express the much desired love they need and by their failure to make the world outside the family understand. These clients speak time after time of picking their father or mother out of the gutter, or always having the house clean and tidy or constantly trying to boost their parents' morale, only to be met by blows, ridicule and a sense of never getting it right.

■ Children's relationships with one another

It is much more common for children in neglectful families to repeat with each other the kind of relationships that their parents engage in than to establish different and more caring relationships. This is not surprising as there are no models of happy relationships for them to imitate. Sadly, children can be as cruel to each other as parents can be to them. They can be aggressive, domineering, sneering, withdrawn and badly neglectful of each other's welfare. Incestuous relationships may also develop between children as they attempt to find some comfort from each other. When children are left with the responsibility of looking after younger siblings they may take out their resentment and anger on their young charges. Children also often blame each other for their parents' moodiness, violence, irritability, drunkenness and hostile silences.

Sometimes, the oldest girl in a neglectful family becomes the parent to the younger children. However, the relationship is more often a dominating and controlling one rather than a caring one and, unfortunately, this often persists into adulthood.

There are neglectful families where the children attempt to protect each other from further hurt and rejection from parents. Over-close relationships can develop and, as adults, major difficulties in separating out from one another can occur.

❑ *Changing neglectful family relationships*

This chapter has described the gross neglect and devastating consequences that are part and parcel of families characterised by absence of care, loveless caring and symbiotic caring. The recipe for changing neglectful family relationships is no different to that outlined in Chapter 2 for changing enmeshed family relationships (see pp. 38–40). However, there is little likelihood that parents of neglectful families will ever adopt these guidelines unless they get guidance and support. It is not that these parents do not want the best for themselves and for their children, quite the contrary. But their poor sense of self and their enormous insecurity make it far too threatening to attempt any change or to reach out to others for help. Because of their inability to seek help themselves, neglectful families usually come to the notice of professional family helpers through schools, family doctors, the police, school-truancy officers, probation officers, social workers, neighbours, the Samaritans, Childline, refuges for women who are victims of violence and rape crisis centres. The help required has to come from professionals (clinical psychologists, family therapists, psychotherapists, psychoanalysts, social workers) who are well versed in family dynamics. Changing neglectful families needs to take account of the many levels of conflict operating within them:

- Conflict of hate and rejection of self within both parents
- Conflict between the two unhappy parents
- Unresolved conflicts within both parents stemming from their families of origin
- The present family conflict that is putting each member at risk
- The conflict within children of their feelings of rejection and their unmet need for love and recognition

Very often such troubled families are in conflict with neighbours, schools, police, employers, in-laws – the web of conflict can be hugely entangled.

The earlier these troubled families are brought for help the better. It is an act of caring to bring such families to the notice of, for example, social workers who have the legal capacity to enter the home; it is an act of neglect to turn a blind eye. The signs and symptoms are not that difficult to see. Teachers are in a remarkably good position to detect signs of neglect early on. A closer liaison between social services and schools would be very valuable in this regard. Relatives, neighbours and visitors to these families are another source of help. It is a cop-out to say 'I don't want to interfere with what is happening in a family.' Who watches out for these children and, indeed, who considers the needs of the hapless couple at the centre of troubled families? It has been my experience that when help is offered in a non-threatening, caring and supportive way there is a positive (though generally guarded) response from even deeply troubled families. Fortunately, there has been a proliferation of helping services for individuals and families who are troubled, and family doctors, teachers, the Samaritans, local social services and Childline will provide the relevant contacts.

CHAPTER 4

Creating the Loving Family

❑ *Unconditional love is the only kind of love*
❑ *Person and behaviour are separate*
❑ *Guidelines for loving family interactions*

Unconditional love corresponds to one of the deepest longings, not only of the child but of every human being.
Erich Fromm

❑ *Unconditional love is the only kind of love*

The essential ingredient in creating the happy family is love. As you have seen in Chapter 2, the most common type of loving shown in families and other social systems is conditional love. This breeds multiple fears, dependencies and self-esteem difficulties within families. By contrast, the loving shown in happy families is unconditional. Whether love is conditional or unconditional is not a benign issue that can be ignored by parents and other leaders of social systems, since any type of loving other than unconditional loving leads to all sorts of problems.

In clinical practice, my experience has been that members of families that are neglectful, emotionless or symbiotic are more likely to develop psychotic manifestations of their inner turmoil, whereas members of families where love is conditional (narcissistic or overprotective) are more likely to manifest neurotic behaviours. This is not surprising because the first three types of family situation are grossly neglectful of family members' welfare, whereas some caring, though conditional, does take place in conditional families and therefore the problems are not as severe. Also, members of families that are totally neglectful feel helpless about ever getting love and recognition, whereas members of conditional families have found some way to gain love, even if it is in a dependent way. The reason why individuals who have experienced conditional love become neurotic in behaviour is that they are fearful, or even sometimes terrified, of not measuring up to the conditions imposed for gaining approval, acceptance and love. There is no strict line between the two main types of family (totally neglectful and conditional) in terms of whether they produce psychotic or neurotic manifestations; it is more a matter of probability. I have worked with people labelled as schizophrenic who came from extremely conditional homes and have worked with members of neglectful families who exhibited obsessional-compulsive behaviours, very high anxiety or deep depressive reactions.

The healthy type of relating that leads to the elevation of the self-esteem of each member of the family and to family togetherness is *empathic relating*. Empathic relating involves unconditional love of the other for her unique being and person and not for anything she does. It is a giving to give rather than to get. The empathic family celebrates each member, allows for the unique growth of each person and provides the resources for such growth. The parents in the empathic family come into their couple relationship and into the family with a high sense of their own worth and a realisation of their own limitations. These parents do not impose their own views on each other or on the children but are sensitive to the unique needs of each other. They show interest in the other's thoughts, feelings, interests, hobbies, spiritual beliefs, philosophy of life, friendships and career because they love the other person. How many parents refuse to go to see their children playing particular sports because they are not of interest to them? How many parents impose their way of doing things on children even though the child may be managing quite well by doing it his own unique way? How many parents dismiss the aspirations of their partners and of their children because they do not fit in with their own aspirations? So many of my clients have talked about having to do things their father's or their mother's way because he or she insisted that that was the 'only right way to do it'. Even when their children are adults, these parents continue to insist on their ways. This is not empathic relating.

There are no conditions for love in the empathic family; love is always present. Relationships come first and they always come before issues relating to responsibilities within the family.

When confrontation or firmness is needed regarding some bit of behaviour, it is done within the context of the loving relationship. The parent in the empathic family can be just as strict and as firm with a child or partner or, indeed, with self about taking responsibility for certain necessary behaviours. Not to be firm would not be loving. However, the person of the other or the relationship with her is never attacked or abused through blaming, criticising, ridiculing or scolding. It is the particular problematic behaviour which is the focus of discussion and while the family member involved will not be allowed to slide out of responsibility, her own person is still loved. The main point about empathic relating is that the relationship with the other is seen as paramount and is not broken because of the irresponsible action.

The children of such a family are typically highly motivated and come to school without having lost their curiosity and desire for learning. In such a family failure and mistakes are treated as opportunities for further learning. Effort is always the focus of encouragement: family members are encouraged to improve their efforts according to their own standards rather than comparing themselves or competing with others. There is no emphasis on performance as every effort is seen as an attainment. The members of an empathic family will be very secure in themselves and will be able to receive feedback on the need for further effort or for greater responsibility without this in any way undermining self-esteem. A child who has these characteristics is a teacher's dream because he listens, works diligently, is not afraid to ask questions and can admit when he does not know or understand something – surely a rare phenomenon in a classroom. There is very little that can rock the security of the child reared in a home-setting of unconditional love. Even a teacher who is conditional or authoritarian will not seriously undermine such a child's self-esteem; here the positive influence of the empathic home will generally override the negative influence of the classroom.

❏ *Person and behaviour are separate*

Keeping person and behaviour separate is an essential aspect of unconditional love and its importance cannot be emphasised enough. It is the aspect of unconditional loving that most people find difficult; this is not surprising as most of us were reared on a diet of conditional loving. When you are subjected to a conditional relationship there is constant confusion between your person and your behaviour. Every human being needs to shout from the rooftops: 'I am not my behaviour', 'I am certainly responsible for my behaviour but no one piece or sequence of behaviour defines my person'. When you label a person as 'lazy', 'no good', 'stupid', 'selfish', 'ugly' or 'aggressive' you are not only rejecting the behaviour but also the person; you are also breaking your relationship with the person and badly affecting the victim's self-esteem. When relating unconditionally, you talk about the behaviour that troubles you, you are firm about not accepting it and you take any necessary action, but you retain your value and respect for the unique person of the family member you are addressing. Where there is unconditional love in the family, the unique person of each member and the relationship between members are always valued far beyond an annoying or troublesome behaviour. Family members are not allowed slide out of responsibility, but the call to responsibility is done in a way that does not damage the person or the relationship.

In the conditional family, the value and worth of a person are evaluated through behaviour. When a parent loves a baby surely it is the fact that the child is unique, breathes, thinks and feels that arouses the love feelings; at this stage there are hardly enough behaviours being shown for one to say that the baby is loved because he shows certain behaviours. It is vital to resolve the confusion between person and behaviour. Whether adult or child, family members are always lovable and worthwhile in their person and nothing, not even the most despicable of behaviours, must take away from that unconditional positive regard.

Behaviour, whether adaptive or maladaptive, is the means by which you try to learn and make sense out of a very complex world. It does not add one jot to your worth as a person. When family members believe their behaviour reflects their importance and worth, they are dependent, trapped, insecure and fearful. For example, a family that believes that it is important and valued, in its own eyes and in the eyes of others, because all its members are medical doctors is highly vulnerable to criticism, loss of status and failure. If families find their value through status, profession and success they are vulnerable and should any of these sources of prestige be lost, then the family may lapse into shame and hopelessness. I remember working with one young man who was deeply unsettled and felt un-accepted by his family and his grandfather (who ruled the roost) because he alone had chosen not to follow the family profession in medicine.

Family members need to enjoy their behaviour, to be chal-lenged by it, to learn and grow in knowledge and wisdom through it, but not to be governed by it. It needs to be con-stantly kept in mind that a family member's worth and value as a person are always separate from anything she does, says, thinks, dreams or feels. Family members have a responsibility to improve behaviour but they cannot improve on their persons, which are perfect and unique.

Main characteristics of unconditional and empathic relating

- Non-possessive warmth and affection
- Non-judgmental attitude
- Separation of person and behaviour
- Demonstration of a love of others and of life
- Regular affirmation of the uniqueness, worth, lovability and capability of each family member
- Sensitivity to and encouragement of each family member's special interests, hobbies and ways of doing things
- Acceptance of each other
- Respect and value for each other
- Acknowledgment of strengths and weaknesses
- An interest in each other's lives
- Active listening
- Encouragement and praise of behavioural efforts
- Development of competition with self not with each other

➡

- Positive firmness with regard to being responsible and positive correction when not responsible
- Family relationships neither threatened nor broken because of unacceptable behaviours
- Genuineness and realness in interactions with one another
- Spontaneity
- Fostering of independence
- Nurturing of creativity
- Absence of comparison of one member with another or with an outsider
- Love of learning and challenge
- Mistakes and failures seen as opportunities for learning

❑ *Guidelines for loving family interactions*

Unconditional love is communicated by means of affirmation, affection, encouragement, concern, support, belief in the other's capability, listening and warmth. It is vital that when family members relate to each other, their interactions are real and genuine.

- *Only ever interact in an honest and genuine way.* If you are not genuine and sincere in your contact and if, for example, you secretly harbour resentment, your non-verbal language (tone of voice, body posture, eye contact, facial expression, gestures) will give you away and your contact with the other will be rejected as insincere.

- *Show love, encouragement, support and belief in the other without expectation of a receptive response.* Generally, it is true to say that when a family member has difficulty in responding to positive contact it means that she needs more unconditional loving. Do not give up when you do not get a positive response; rather hold on to the realisation that the love of and belief in the other shown by you is a revelation of something you feel and perceive, and must not be expressed in order to gain a particular response (otherwise it is both conditional and manipulative). At some point the family member will perceive your honesty and sincerity, and will be affirmed by it.

- *The best act of love is undivided attention.* Avoid effusive expressions of love which are rarely sincere. A look, a nod, a smile or a touch may be sufficient to affirm a family member. When communicating always be sure to give your full attention.

- *Be sure your contact with the other is unconditional and has no ulterior motive.* Do not give to get, whether you are giving affection, praise, affirmation, encouragement, support or help. When you look for something in return you are not loving the other but are attempting to manipulate and, consequently, the interaction will have negative consequences.

- *Do not use clichés, jargon and popular superlatives.* Examples are: 'Great', 'Out of this world', 'A1', 'Fab', 'Super'; these are rarely believed. Be yourself and be sincere and genuine.

- *Spontaneous expressions of praise, affirmation and encouragement are the most powerful means of communicating love.* The surprise gift, embrace, affirmation, expression of happiness and warmth are treasures that are far too rarely found in family members' interactions with each other.

- *Focus some of your affection, praise or encouragement on areas that are important to the particular family member.* Look for signs from family members of what is important to them. Possible areas are physical appearance, dress, work, garden, sports, reading, career, music, literature, friendships. Pay heed also to what you hear from a family member's friends, teachers, colleagues and relations.

- *Distinguish between affirmation and praise in your contact with another.* Many family members confuse affirmation with praise. An affirmation values some unique aspect of a family member such as her way of seeing things, creative way of doing something, dress sense, physical looks, way of looking, smiling and so on. Praise focuses on some action such as doing school homework well, helping with the wash-up, fixing an electrical fault, tidying a room, mowing the lawn and so on. It is best to praise the effort in the action rather than the performance outcome of the action.

All family members have a need for recognition and approval. Recognition, respect, valuing, affirmation, praise and encouragement are not often regular features of interactions between family members. It is the responsibility of all family members to develop a climate of positive interactions based on these guidelines. Unconditional loving is a subtle, delicate matter but when it occurs it has many rewarding consequences. Finally, it needs to be realised that unconditional loving is an act of will. It is easy to be loving when all is well within the family; the real test is when the going gets difficult. When this happens, genuine, sincere and regular acts of unconditional loving will serve to resolve issues much more quickly.

CHAPTER 5

Resolving Family Conflicts

❏ *Conflict is positive!*
- Physical change
- Behavioural change
- Emotional change
- Social change
- Sexual change
- Cognitive change

❏ *Problem-solving approach to resolving family conflicts*
- Identification of the problem
- Communication of the conflict
- Brainstorming solutions
- Selection of a solution
- Action
- Monitoring progress of action
- Evaluation of conflict-solving strategy

Always remember that no matter what the problem may be, there is an infinity of solutions.
Marian Weinstein

❏ *Conflict is positive!*

Conflict can be a creative force within a family (or any other social system) when it is seen as an opportunity for change. The presence of conflict within a family acts as a signal to its members that some healing process is required and if this signal is heeded then family harmony can be attained. This healing process may be required at different levels:

- physical
- behavioural
- emotional

69

- social
- sexual
- cognitive.

■ Physical change

Sometimes conflict arises within a family to bring attention to the fact that a member is physically ill and requires medical attention, rest or some relief from responsibilities. A child who is cranky is very often showing signs of a cold, 'flu' or earache. A mother who is irritable may be tired or physically over-burdened; she may be experiencing pre-menstrual tension or may have some physical infection; she may even be showing signs of more serious illness. A father who is being aggressive may be showing the ill-effects of excessive alcohol intake or overwork. In effective families the physical remedies to these conflicts are quickly introduced and harmony is restored. In ineffective families the symptoms either go unnoticed or are reacted to with impatience, irritability or withdrawal. The conflict increases as a consequence and sometimes has to get to 'screaming point' – serious illness, physical breakdown, violence – before something is done. All the time the purpose of the conflict is for the unmet physical needs to be seen, heard and met.

■ Behavioural change

Many conflicts within families arise because there is poor or no behavioural control within and between the family members. Examples of lack of behavioural control are: shouting, scream-ing, hitting, kicking, grabbing, pushing, shoving, carelessness, poor hygiene, neglect of each other's property, unhealthy eating and drinking, dominating, controlling, blaming, criticising. Each of these behaviours leads either to reactions of a similar nature and a vicious cycle of 'tit for tat' or to physical or emotional withdrawal. Both the 'out-of-control' behaviour and the reactions to it are clear manifestations of the behavioural healing that is needed within the family. Out-of-control be-haviours are usually indicators of deeper emotional issues that need to be resolved. Nonetheless, some reduction of these behaviours is necessary to facilitate work on the hidden issues of fears of criticism, rejection, failure, dependence on others and poor sense of self. One of the initial steps for families in conflict is to take control of these protective out-of-control behaviours. The absence of violence, criticism, scolding, ridicule, 'put-down' messages, sarcasm, cynicism and verbal aggression makes it easier to establish the presence of love, respect, value, affirmation, praise, care, listening, compassion, understanding, humour and fairness between members of a family. Sometimes, behavioural problems reflect the absence of parenting skills. Behavioural control is a major issue within families and is dealt with in more detail in Chapter 9.

▪ Emotional change

When families relate in ways that are neglectful or conditional, all sorts of conflicts manifest themselves. Once again these conflicts are signs that emotional healing is needed within the family.

Signs of emotional conflict	
• Psychosomatic signs	Asthma • arthritis • back pain • tension headaches • stomach ulcers • abdominal pain • cancer • heart disease • hypertension
• Behavioural signs	Aggression • blaming • violence • physical withdrawal or abuse • clinging • possessiveness • perfectionism • passivity • compulsive actions
• Affective signs	No display of warmth, closeness, affection, compassion or affirmation • suppression of feelings of fear, sadness or loneliness • depression • repression of feelings • rejection • irritability • over-expression of feelings of love, caring and attention

→

• Cognitive signs	Overabsorption in interests and hobbies • overstudying • intellectualising of emotional problems • obsessions with cleanliness, values or religion • 'living in one's head' • delusions • hallucinations • depressive and anxious thought patterns • 'living in the future' • 'living in the past' • scruples
• Social signs	Few or no couple or family outings • few visits to the family from outsiders • little or no conversation • shyness • social phobias of meeting people or public speaking • silences that can go on for weeks or months • people-pleasing • inability to say 'no' • family member always out with others • non-listening • non-stop talking
• Sexual signs	Little or no sexual contact between couple • male partner has impotency problems or premature ejaculation • female partner has vaginismus or is non-orgasmic • excessive masturbation by young children • incest • sexual abuse • confusion regarding sexual identity

Many emotional problems within families manifest themselves through sexual behaviours. I have worked with children who were sexual with each other in the family or with others outside the family in a subconscious attempt to gain contact that showed they were wanted. Fathers may sexually abuse their daughters because they have no sexual confidence with adults or because they lack love of themselves and feel rejected by their partners. This is not an excuse for their abusive actions but little healing can happen if deeper understanding of and response to their hidden conflicts does not occur. A man's sexual impotency may be a manifestation of his sense of powerlessness around women. A woman's difficulty in allowing sexual penetration may be a revelation of her fear of intimacy and closeness. A child's excessive masturbation may indicate a need for love, affection and physical holding. It may also reveal excessive pressure from emotional turmoil (for example, fear of parents' hitting out or shouting) within the child with the self-stimulation acting to relieve (temporarily) some of the pressure.

Resolving emotional problems within a family can be a lengthy process as the problems may be deep-seated and may have their sources in the families of origin of the parents. Some troubled parents have not themselves separated out from their own parents and return frequently to their original homes in a vain effort to get the recognition, acceptance and love they did not get as children. Sadly, in remaining dependent on their parents they neglect their own marriage and their own family. The cycle of neglect and rejection repeats itself, not because of any genetic influence, but because the unresolved childhood conflicts of the parents take a heavy emotional toll on partner and children. In my experience the following are essential aspects of emotional healing within a family:

- Separation of each parent from family of origin
- Establishment of each parent's own identity
- Development by the parents of independence of others' opinions and perceptions and of their own behavioural performance
- Development of an unconditionally loving, supportive, valuing, respectful, fair, just and friendly relationship between the parents
- Creation of an empathic relationship between the parents and children
- Particular attention to the development of the self-esteem of each child
- An understanding that problems and conflicts always are opportunities for change within the family

Separating out from family of origin is an essential first step for many parents and also for adults who are still living at home with parents or who travel home virtually every weekend. Non-separateness reveals a continuing high dependence on parents' approval, acceptance and recognition, and an absence of self-regard. Because parents in the family of origin themselves have low self-esteem, it is unlikely that going back to them will ever get the needed response to unmet childhood needs; and even if it does, the danger is that the adult child will continue to be dependent on the parents. As an adult, you are your own primary source of love, approval and acceptance; it is simply a lovely bonus if these are shown to you by others.

I once worked with a man in his late thirties who was married with one child and who travelled forty miles every day to see his mother – a woman who had never shown him affection, affirmation or praise. She related to him in the classic narcissistic way, seeing only her own needs. It was sad to see how his poor self-esteem was affecting his own family. His wife felt that his mother was more important to him than she was and there were many arguments over his visits. She felt rejected but rather than saying this she resorted to blaming him and his 'selfish dominating mother'. His three-year-old daughter was also being affected, as on return from work he would incessantly question her:

- 'Did you miss your Daddy today?'
- 'How many times did you think of your Daddy today?'
- 'Were you lonely without Daddy?'
- 'Do you love your Daddy?'
- 'Are you sure you love your Daddy?'
- 'How do you know you love your Daddy?'

All these questions revealed his inner conviction that nobody could really love him. His daughter was becoming deeply insecure because her love for him was being doubted. His wife told me that the child used to watch and wait for her father's return from work (and from his mother's house), sometimes for hours, and on sight of him coming into the driveway, she would run out waving frantically and shouting repeatedly 'Daddy, Daddy, I love you'.

Separateness means joining with yourself through a celebration of your own unique being and cutting the ties of dependence that bind you to parents and others. Separateness has nothing to do with geographical distance: some people may emigrate and still be dependent on their parents – their insecurity simply is displaced onto others who become their substitute parents. Giving yourself acceptance, recognition, praise, affirmation, caring and nurturance and being independent of the reaction of others towards you is the way to separate out from parents and others.

Many people confuse independence with meeting needs and question how you can be totally independent when many of your needs are met in relationships with others. Since we are social beings it is true that many of our needs – emotional, sexual, social, medical, physical, educational – are met through relationships with others. Being independent does not mean denying these needs; rather it means letting the other person know what your need is but without insistence that your need be met and without feelings of rejection if it is not met. You are responsible for your own needs, not the other person; that person is entitled to say 'yes' or 'no' to your requests. If one person is not willing or able to meet your need then there may be somebody else who can respond and, if not, then maybe you can do something yourself. But some people cannot accept a 'no' and either react aggressively and dismissively or go into a sulk. Either way they are showing dependence on the reaction of the other. By behaving defensively, they harm their relationship with the person who said 'no'; they further undermine their own and the other person's self-esteem; and they make it very difficult for themselves to make future requests. Pseudo-independence, on the other hand, is never asking for anything. The person who does this is seriously dependent as the real reason he does not make requests is the fear that others will see him as weak, vulnerable or needy and will reject him – in other words he is very much dependent on the approval of others. True independence means asking for whatever you want, allowing the other person freedom to respond or not to respond, and realising that, as an adult, you are responsible for yourself.

■ Social change

It is pointed out above that social excesses or deficits within a family may be signs of deeper emotional problems. However, some family conflicts are purely socially based, arising from lack of sensitivity to social needs or lack of social skills within the family. Because of stereotyping many men have seen the place of their female partners as being in the bed, in the kitchen and in the church. These men, and very often their spouses also, did not realise that women need social stimulation for their ongoing personal development. Research has shown that housebound women are much more prone to depression than women who have career and social outlets.

Many adults and children find it difficult to create relationships because of not knowing the basic ways to introduce oneself, to initiate and maintain conversation, to identify the body language of others, to express needs, feelings and so on. Teaching basic social skills to people with social deficits can add enormously to their emotional and social development.

The child who is socially skilled adapts with ease to new situations whereas the child who is painfully shy encounters untold problems. Very often a child lacks the social skills because the parents themselves are not great socialisers and, therefore, do not provide the child with the appropriate modelling of social skills and the opportunities to practise them.

Lack of family outings and family time within the home are sometimes issues that need to be tackled within a problematic family. The more family members interact with one another the greater the cohesiveness and the closeness within that family. It was once a catch-cry in this country that 'the family who prays together stays together'. But, it takes more than one type of interaction to create bonds between family members. The following are some examples of what is needed:

- Listening
- Helping
- Sharing
- Playing
- Games
- Humour

- Interest in each other
- Problem-solving
- Planning
- Outings
- Parties

■ Sexual change

Most sexual problems within a relationship are due to underlying relationship problems or even deeper self-esteem difficulties. However, some sexual problems are purely a matter of ignorance where the couple do not know ways to sexually pleasure each other. In this case, an increase in sexual expertise can greatly enhance the sexual relationship. There are numerous books and videos offering such knowledge.

It is interesting that most adolescents will talk with their parents on any subject except sex. A taboo around sex still exists in many families. This means that children grow up with either misinformation or no information, and may experience confusion and guilt when they begin to notice body changes and sexual urges. Many young people and adults still have a lot of guilt about self-stimulation; they are not aware that at least 90 per cent of people masturbate, even though, unfortunately, only 1 per cent may admit to it. Some sexual problems then may be a result of lack of knowledge and it is important that parents first of all educate themselves and then their children on the pleasures of responsible sexuality.

■ Cognitive change

Many people exacerbate problems through 'brooding'; they are like children picking at a scab. These people need to be encouraged to talk about what is happening and to say what their needs are. Critical self-talk is a cognitive behaviour that undermines confidence. Typical examples of this are:

- 'I wish I didn't have to do this.'
- 'Do we really have to meet these people?'
- 'I know I'll just make a fool of myself.'
- 'Look at the state of me.'
- 'I hate myself.'
- 'I look terrible.'
- 'I know I'll fail that exam.'
- 'Why am I not like other people?'

Children as well as adults engage in critical self-talk. Parents need to teach themselves and their children to be encouraging and positive in the way they talk to themselves so that they build up their confidence. It is known that children who read poorly see themselves in terms of the label 'poor readers'. Many adults have a mind-set that says 'I'm no good at mathematics'. Well, if that is what you tell yourself then that is what the outcome will be. However, if you tell yourself, 'I have all the resources to learn this subject and by regularly applying myself I can learn', you are more likely to attain at the subject. Motivation is often blocked by the critical thoughts that go on in adults' and children's heads.

Feelings of resentment, anger, jealousy, envy and fear can also be fuelled by thoughts of revenge, by reliving old hurts, by anticipation of failure, by rehearsal of one's 'faults' and so on. Correction of these thinking patterns serves to keep the original emotional issue in perspective. Many books have been written on positive thinking. My own view is that the practice of such thoughts is certainly of help but unless the underlying issues of low self-esteem and problematic family relationships are resolved, it is unlikely that just changing cognitive patterns will be of lasting value.

Lack of parenting, educational and domestic skills can be a serious cognitive deficit leading to conflict within a family. Acquiring these skills is a prerequisite to effective parenting. Unfortunately it is parents with low self-esteem who are much more likely to lack knowledge and skills, but these are also the people who are unlikely to venture out to gain such information unless some shift occurs in their level of self-esteem. Very often, in courses on parenting skills, one is speaking to the converted and the absence of those who most need the course is noticeable. Children also often lack information; a sensitivity to that deficit and the creation of opportunities for learning will benefit their ongoing intellectual and emotional development.

❑ *Problem-solving approach to resolving family conflicts*

It is interesting that when healthy families are faced with conflict they go through a series of action stages to resolve it, whereas in unhealthy families even the first step of problem-solving may not be carried through. There are different problem-solving methods; the one suggested below is a seven-step method.

■ Identification of the problem

It is useful to categorise problems as *instrumental* and *affective*. Instrumental difficulties are connected with resources and responsibilities within the family. Typical instrumental family conflicts involve shortage of money and who cooks, shops, cleans, washes, brings in fuel, does the garden, walks the dog, spring cleans the house and so on. Affective conflicts include personal and interpersonal emotional and behavioural problems of family members. Examples of these are a parent who is fretful, anxious or depressed, a parent who is dependent on alcohol or prescribed drugs, a child who is shy, timid, anxious or withdrawn, or a situation where there is excessive silence or aggression within a family.

An important element of this first step in problem-solving is 'who' actually identifies the problem. A child who attempts to do so sometimes may not be taken seriously and may even be dismissed or punished for revealing the conflict issue. To some extent the Childline phone service has given children some medium through which they can seek help for serious conflict situations. Teachers and close relatives are an ideal source of help for children who are troubled but, unfortunately, some adults have the notion that you should not interfere in another family's affairs. It is true that when someone outside the family identifies the problem the parents are usually quite resistant to being helped. However, when children are at risk, action must be taken if parents fail to take responsibility. This may mean, for example, an approach to the family by a teacher or the visit of a social worker who has a legal right to check on the safety and welfare of all family members. When nothing is done about family conflict everybody loses out – the parents, the marriage, the family, the children, the school, the community and society.

Instrumental problems tend to be far more frequently identified within a family than affective problems. The latter are more threatening to self-esteem and, consequently, are denied, suppressed or projected onto others. Sometimes, a strong emotional reaction may be shown to instrumental issues – for example, being on time for meals or taking turns to do the wash-up – which masks deeper affective conflict within the family

such as one partner not feeling wanted, a child feeling burdened
with adult responsibilities or a mother feeling dominated and
controlled by her partner. I recall the case of a twelve-year-old
girl who daily used to plunge herself, fully clothed, into the
river at the bottom of the garden, no matter what time of the
year it was. All sorts of threats and promises failed to change
the behaviour. Her mother regarded her as being 'stubborn
and bold' while her father was silent on the matter. Eventually,
when she was brought for help I discovered from the child that
she was being sexually abused by her father. The plunging into
the cold river was a subconscious attempt to 'freeze' her
feelings of disgust, anger and hate and also an attempt to cleanse
herself because she saw her body as polluted.

The important factor to watch out for when a problem is
identified – whether affective or instrumental – is the emotional
'loading' that surrounds the problem; this is primarily expressed
in non-verbal language. Examples of these non-verbal signs
are facial expression, tone of voice, loudness of voice, nervous
mannerisms, eye contact and body posture. It is important to
try to get to the feelings behind the family member's reaction
as these reveal the seriousness of the issue for him.

- ■ Communication of the conflict

Attempts at conflict resolution often falter at the second step
of problem-solving. Very often, even though the problem has
been identified, nothing happens because the parent or child
or outsider who identified the problem says nothing. For
example, many spouses and children never reveal the physical,
emotional or sexual abuse they may be experiencing at the
hands of a family member or some relative, neighbour or child-
minder. The emotional safety has not been created within the
family which would enable its members to reveal whatever
personal, interpersonal or instrumental problems are occurring.
Apart from the situation where nothing at all is done, other
non-productive actions following problem identification include
gossip, blaming, complaining, withdrawal into hostile silence
and resignation to the fact that nothing can be done. All of these
responses serve only to escalate the existing conflict. When a

problem is isolated it is expedient that it is communicated to a person who can help. Everybody benefits when a conflict is challenged.

■ Brainstorming solutions

Brainstorming solutions is the most creative and dynamic stage in conflict resolution. This is when the family members get together and look for ways of resolving the conflict; the strategy is to express whatever idea comes into your head that might resolve the problem. It is important that all family members who have reached the age of language and reason be involved. Unfortunately children or adolescents are often not included in this process even though its outcome may directly affect them. When there are in-laws living within the home they should also be included. 'Whispering' or 'secret' meetings tend to create insecurity and are always a threat to the self-esteem of the person excluded from the meeting. There must be no judgment or criticism of proffered solutions during brainstorming no matter how ridiculous another participant may feel they are. Any judgment will quickly dry up creativity as family members will not be willing to risk the humiliation of being ridiculed. It is easy to see how a verbal judgment such as 'that's so stupid' will sabotage brainstorming but much more subtle non-verbal messages, like sighing, tut-tutting, grimacing, turning one's eyes heavenwards or winking to another, can be equally devastating. All solutions should be written down and all efforts encouraged and affirmed.

■ Selection of a solution

Selection of a solution can be the most difficult step as any differences between family members are much more likely to occur at this stage. It is always difficult to select a solution that will suit everybody. Because of this, entrenched positions can often be taken. Consideration of two issues will make it less likely that such a stalemate will emerge:

- what is to be done (the instrumental factor)?
- who will benefit from a commitment to the proposed solution (the affective or relationship factor)?

If the family considers only the 'what' of the problem, individual members may be resistant to taking on more responsibilities. However, if relationships are also considered they are much more likely to be amenable to adopting a solution that may be of considerable help to another in the family. For example, it may be difficult for family members to accept that each needs to take more responsibility for certain household tasks until they consider the affective issue and see how their helping will mean that mother will be less tired and depressed and will feel more valued. A family member who does not respond to the emotional needs of another seriously needs to ask himself: 'What is blocking me from helping another family member who is in obvious distress?' Very often the answer to that question will bring up the unmet needs of the person asking the question. This then is a further opportunity for growth within the family.

■ Action

The action stage is the most important one, as all the words in the world may not change conflict situations but actions can and do. Some families go through the earlier steps but then nothing happens or only half-hearted attempts are made or perhaps commendable efforts are initiated but not maintained. To guard against such an outcome it is wise to introduce an accountability system. This is not a policing system but a method of ensuring the continuance of action on the problems occurring within the family through support, encouragement and feedback. The procedure is to divide out responsibility for the action plan between individual family members or groups of family members and arrange meetings at set times and places so that reports can be given to each other on progress and on any difficulties that may have arisen. This accountability system needs to be well organised and executed.

■ Monitoring progress of action

Following action, the question then has to be asked: is the solution chosen having any effect on the family conflict? It may be that family members are truly trying but little or no change has occurred over the last weeks. It may be that more or different action is needed; if it is the latter then a return to the fourth step is needed for the selection of another option. If, on the implementation of this new solution, nothing much happens, then it may be that the family is looking at the wrong problem or only at a surface issue which is masking a much deeper affective problem. In this case, a return to the first step is required to identify the real conflict issue.

■ Evaluation of conflict-solving strategy

The main aim of this final stage is to bring the lessons of the present conflict-resolution experience into the resolution of problems which will inevitably arise in the future. Families will never be totally without conflicts. New conflicts will arise in response to the continuing self-esteem difficulties of family members and also in response to the developmental cycle of a family. This goes from a couple relationship, to a family with young children, to a family with adolescents, to a family with young adults separating out to make their own independent lives, to a middle-age couple left alone again and finally to one of the spouses remaining alone following the death of the partner. Each stage of this cycle brings different instrumental and affective demands and some of these can lead to conflict between family members. A common conflict nowadays is 'who will look after an ageing parent?' Previous experience of tackling difficulties helps with future conflict resolution when the insights and effective strategies developed are brought to bear on the new conflict. Beware though of assuming that what worked before will always work again.

CHAPTER 6

Meeting Needs within the Family

❑ *Needs and family development*
❑ *Needs of individual family members*
❑ *Needs of the couple*
❑ *Needs of the family*
❑ *Confrontation on unmet needs*

> *I like not only to be loved, but also to be told*
> *that I am loved . . . the realm of silence*
> *is large enough beyond the grave.*
> George Eliot

❑ *Needs and family development*

The primary function of the family is the optimum development of each member. The meeting of the reasonable and basic needs of each family member is the cornerstone of individual fulfilment. This responsibility needs to be shared out and as children grow older they need to be firmly encouraged to take on more and more responsibility for meeting their own needs. The major responsibility is to own your needs and not expect others to be able to read your mind. Some typical ways in which couples communicate about needs are:

- 'You never consider my needs.'
- 'You only always think about yourself.'
- 'You're so selfish.'

The partner who is complaining and blaming in these examples will rarely have actually expressed her needs. When reasonable needs have been expressed and no fair response is forthcoming, then confrontation is required.

Clearly, needs may differ between families, cultures and geographical locations. However the needs of family members outlined below are those which are basic and essential both to the mature development of each family member and to the establishment of family harmony, irrespective of culture, wealth, class, education or geographical location.

❑ *Needs of individual family members*

During the first two to three years of life children are totally dependent on parents to meet their needs. Once they develop language or can understand instructions they can be shown how to meet more and more of their needs by themselves. Certainly by early adolescence they should be able to do many things for themselves, for example cook, tidy room, wash, study without supervision, dress well, be hygienic, shop for self, clean house, do garden, iron own clothes, affirm and encourage self. Their early experiences will determine their later ability to be responsible. In these early years parents have a major responsibility to respond to the multiple needs of their children and to ensure that they learn gradually to develop responsibility for themselves. The way that parents meet their own and children's needs forms the model that the children will adopt later on in meeting their needs themselves. Therefore, if children's needs are neglected by parents then this pattern of neglect may well be repeated by the children in later adolescence and adulthood. Equally, if parents overindulge and overprotect children then they will lack the ability to care for themselves later on and will continue to look to others to be responsible for them. There is a healthy middle ground between these two extremes. Parents need to be aware of the following basic needs of children and of themselves if they are to fulfil this responsibility.

Checklist of needs of individual family members
• Need for love and affection • Need to feel wanted • Need for assurance against abandonment • Need for positive experiences →

- Need for respect
- Need for protection
- Need for limits
- Need for security
- Need for belief in each other's capabilities
- Need for challenge
- Need for guidance and consultation
- Need for self-determination
- Need for freedom
- Need for self-confidence
- Need for a sense of humour

■ Need for love and affection

The need for love and affection is the most important need of children and indeed of all family members; it is what is wanted more than anything else. In regard to this need, particularly in the case of young children (and not so young!), actions always speak louder than words. Children need both to be told and to be shown that they are loved. The most powerful way to demonstrate warmth and affection is by natural and spontaneous physical contact – the hug, the embrace, the pat on the back, the hand in the hand or on the shoulder, the silent holding. Being involved in what the child or adult is doing is yet another way of showing affection.

■ Need to feel wanted

Family members need to know that their presence or absence from the family matters and is noted. At all times they need to feel they are wanted and that no action on their part detracts from that sense of being wanted. When family members are given attention when they need it, are accepted when they get things wrong and are treated with generous affection, they will feel genuinely and sincerely wanted. Sometimes, because of their own limitations parents scold and ridicule children, leading them to feel unwanted. If the parent in this case, having regained composure, can go to the child, apologise for the loss of temper and express love for the child then the child will quickly regain security about feeling wanted.

■ Need for assurance against abandonment

This need is much more manifest in younger children but adolescents and adults can also show deep fears of abandonment by others, especially those closest to them. I get very disturbed when I hear parents threatening children with such statements as:

- 'I wish I never had you.'
- 'Sometimes, I feel like giving you away.'
- 'If you're not good, I may not be here in the morning.'
- 'You're just endless trouble to me.'
- 'I don't know why I put up with you?'

All these threats feed into children's terror of being abandoned, a terror which springs from the fact that children are totally dependent on parents. Many parents witness this fear, for example, when they go to have an evening out together and are leaving the child with a babysitter and the child screams the house down to make the parents stay. The parents know they will return but the child is not an adult and the fear of the parents not returning is dominating his behaviour at the moment of their departure. It would be unwise for them to stay home in reaction to the child's fear and it is important to realise that when children are gradually conditioned to the goings and comings of parents this fear subsides. Once children have a basic level of language, parents can let them know in advance when they are going, for how long and when the children can expect to see them return. They can also ring and let them know if they are going to be late. It is well for parents to remember that later on they may be the ones sitting at home wondering where their adolescent son is and when he will return. If parents understand their children's fears and respond appropriately, it is more likely that they will be accorded the same understanding and sensitivity later on.

A parent can also suffer fears of rejection and can demonstrate extreme behaviours when the possibility of rejection is
present. Such parents need to learn to be there for themselves
and to become independent of their partners and children.

■ Need for positive experiences

Parenting is an extremely difficult task and there are tendencies
in all of us to be negative in our outlook at times. But being
exposed to negative attitudes can lead children to view life as
a miserable rather than an enjoyable and positive experience.
Many children have experienced and unfortunately sometimes
still experience much misery in classrooms due to the mis-
guided notion that children should be beaten (verbally and
physically) into being responsible. Many parents also still hold
this belief. They believe that being aggressive, dominating,
controlling, verbally abusive, critical, condemning, scolding
and ridiculing are the means to rearing children effectively.
Nothing is further from the truth. Children who experience
such negative interactions rarely get past the conviction that
life is miserable and unhappy. Avoidance, rebelliousness,
apathy or perfectionism are all characteristics of these children
later on in life. There needs to be:

* an absence of physical abuse, ridiculing, scolding, criticism,
  cynicism, sarcasm, comparison with others – anything
  that damages children's belief in themselves, in others
  and in life
* the presence of love, affection, praise, encouragement,
  recognition, acceptance and affirmation – everything that
  heightens children's belief in themselves, in others and
  in life.

Fair treatment, encouragement, positive receptivity to mistakes and failure, and firm but positive correction of irresponsible actions all set the ground for children to maximise their
potential. It is important to help children to see that mistakes
and failures are opportunities for further learning of knowledge
and skills and are no reflection whatsoever on their vast
potential for learning. Inevitably, children encounter difficulties

in relationships, in schoolwork, in games and in acquiring self-help skills; their parents need to help them to develop positive ways of dealing with their everyday problems.

The need for positive experiences is also critical to the relationship between parents and between children and parents. It is important to constantly attempt to meet this need in these relationships.

■ Need for respect

The word 'respect' means to consider another 'worthy of esteem'. Children, adolescents and adults alike need the respect of other family members and the considerate treatment that goes with it if each is to form a positive sense of self. As most people are unsure of themselves their feelings can be easily hurt. When children, particularly, experience any slight it tends to magnify and confirm their worst fear about themselves. This would only be a minor issue if slights to children (and others) were uncommon but unfortunately the opposite is true. Children, generally, are seen as less important and less significant than adults and adult concerns. This attitude is reflected in the popular saying 'Children should be seen and not heard'. Children already disadvantaged by age, size, inexperience and their own doubts about themselves are further handicapped by being given second-class regard. Such treatment can only increase their feelings of self-doubt and block their emotional and social development.

As a parent you need to give children the same kind of consideration you give to adults or expect for yourself. Whenever practicable, do not interrupt a conversation with your child because somebody older wants your attention. Try not to make your child wait longer for something than you would reasonably expect yourself to wait. The essential issue here is to give children the same consideration you would expect for yourself or give to any worthwhile person.

■ Need for protection

Helplessness may be children's first emotional experience. Suddenly, at birth, they find themselves exiting from a warm, dimly lit place, where all their needs were being met, to an unknown environment where they are totally dependent on others for their most elementary needs. To a great extent, the task of parenting is helping children to grow from this level of helplessness to becoming powerful and self-reliant enough to meet their own needs. In the meantime, children need protection against their feelings of helplessness.

The protection that children need from physical dangers in the environment is quite apparent to most parents: you strap young children into high chairs, you put a gate at the top and bottom of the stairs to stop children from falling downstairs or climbing upstairs, you ensure exits from front and back gardens are secured, you put a fire guard in the fireplace, you keep sharp instruments out of children's way and so on. As children become more able to recognise these dangers and protect themselves from them you remove these safeguards.

What is less obvious to many parents are the emotional and social dangers that children encounter and, unless parents are vigilant, children may tend to avoid challenges that involve such perils. For example, going to school, developing new friendships, joining a sports club, tackling new areas of knowledge, telling the truth – all of these challenges involve emotional risk-taking that children need to be enabled to face. The risks include:

- 'Will I be liked by the teacher and other pupils?'
- 'Will I be as good as other children at my lessons?'
- 'Will I be rejected when I attempt to find a new friend?'
- 'Will I be popular with other children in the team?'
- 'Will I fail?'
- 'Will I be punished for revealing the truth?'

Parents are often unaware of these fears that are very real to children. Indeed, such fears are common to adults as well and to protect ourselves we often blind ourselves to these vulnerabilities and do likewise when children show similar problems. When that happens, children may be allowed to get away with avoiding many essential challenges and, in the process, miss the chance to grow.

The parents' role here is to provide the emotional support and protection that children need in order to take on these challenges. Adults also need to provide support and understanding for each other when they have similar fears. It is important that adults do not collude with avoidance behaviours on the part of any family member – partner, adolescent or young child – because collusion is overprotection and, unfortunately, only serves to maintain helplessness. Encouragement, support, belief in the ability of the other, and fostering of independence of success, failure and others' opinions are what create the launch pad for facing life's challenges.

■ Need for limits

One of the saddest revelations for children is that the world does not revolve around them. Even when they begin to discover this they tend to hold on to the belief that it should. Children will take things belonging to other family members without asking permission or will wander down the road or call to a neighbour's house, not realising how upsetting it can be for parents who do not know where they are. Not surprisingly, these behaviours eventually get them into trouble. Children learn their limits by making mistakes. There are many ways that parents can help children to reduce the number and the severity of these mistakes:

- Explore the possible repercussions of certain behaviours in advance of their occurrence
- Help children to learn from situations where they did not anticipate punishing consequences
- Lay down clear and fair rules, and be predictable and consistent in their enforcement

Parents also need to set clear limits between each other, for example, rights to privacy and to having one's own opinions, making requests rather than commands of each other, fair sharing of resources and so on. These clear and fair limits in the parental relationship serve as a model for children of how they cannot have everything they want, when they want it, without consideration of the needs of others.

■ Need for security

Security is the feeling that comes from unconditional loving which communicates to each member of the family that: 'You are accepted and valued for being who you are and not for what you do.' This unconditional acceptance of the person of each family member is what gives children and adults the confidence to learn from mistakes, failures and feelings of inadequacy. Family members need desperately to know that they will be accepted even:

- If I don't get that job promotion or raise in salary
- If I don't bring home a report card showing high achievements
- If I do not get on the school (or senior) team
- If I burn the dinner
- If I make mistakes
- If I say 'no' to requests
- If I want to visit my home of origin

The issue of not breaking the relationship because of particular behaviours is a crucial one for the security of all family members. Through the security of acceptance of each other, family members are given the independence to face their own weaknesses and life's challenges. When family members do not experience such acceptance they become tentative, fearful or pessimistic, lack confidence and feel chronically insecure.

■ Need for belief in each other's capabilities

As human beings we have limitless capacity but few people know or are told this. Children and adults alike have severe doubts about their capability and their social acceptability. When these doubts are present, family members are very vulnerable to ridicule, criticism and rejection. They can be made to feel worthless, useless and incompetent if frequently reminded of failures and shortcomings. When, on the other hand, family members are frequently reminded of their immeasurable capacity to learn and their unique presence, they will feel valued, capable and worthwhile. Recall for yourself how powerfully an encouraging word can lift your hopes, your competence and your confidence. Such encouragement of each other can never occur too often within the family.

■ Need for challenge

About 10 per cent of elderly people cannot be distinguished physically, emotionally, socially, intellectually or creatively from young people. The secret to the aliveness of these elderly people is that they sought out challenges throughout life. Challenge is the fuel that keeps the engine of life running smoothly and efficiently. Children and adults need to form the habit of seeking and making challenges, so that they and their families can mature emotionally, socially and educationally. Because challenges are not easy, nor always exciting, the danger is that family members will attempt to avoid the effort required. When parents themselves show a love of learning and a willingness to take on other challenges children will often follow suit. However, this does not always occur and so parents need to be vigilant and to frequently set challenges for the child. It is important to remember what counts most of all is responsible effort and not performance. Once children, with the help of encouragement and positive firmness, maintain efforts they will gain the knowledge, skills and social acceptance that they need. The stakes here are high: if children (or adults) are allowed to avoid necessary life challenges, they and the family will be condemned to a difficult life.

Undoubtedly, when parents challenge children to make efforts, the children may often regard the parents as 'nags' and 'grumblers', but this is a small price to pay. Parents need to accept such reactions with good humour but nevertheless to maintain firmness. Children need to know that allowing them to slide out of responsibility would mean not loving them. But this process always has to be carried out within the context of an unconditional and supportive relationship.

■ Need for guidance and consultation

There are times within every family when one member or another needs knowledge on a particular issue or advice regarding a decision that has to be made or time for consultation on an issue. These needs are especially prominent in children as many of their difficulties are caused by a simple lack of information or lack of skills. Young children believe that parents know everything, and if parents make themselves available and approachable their children will consult them frequently. In contrast, adolescents are inclined to believe that parents know nothing. Giving advice to children, or indeed to adolescents or adults, requires a sensitivity to the other person's vulnerability. It is vital to show respect for the feelings expressed and for the other person's view of the problem.

Parents have many life experiences under their belt and their children can benefit greatly from this. It is important, however, that whatever the situation – whether parents with children, or parent with parent, or adolescent with younger sibling – the person being consulted does not impose her point of view. People must not feel obliged to follow the advice given; otherwise advising becomes commanding. When there is pressure to follow the advice given it is less likely that members of the family will go to each other for help. A good rule of thumb is: only give advice when asked. Certainly, it is important to show concern if you feel that a family member is upset, sad, withdrawn or angry, but it is more productive to say something like 'I'm concerned that you seem upset and I'm wondering is there anything I can do to help?' than to question the other person ('what's wrong with you?') or make judgments about what should be done ('what you need to do is to go away out for yourself'). When you do not have the answer or do not know how to help, it is best to simply admit it. This equalises the relationship and the fact that you are honest will make it easier for the other person, when in need, to approach you again.

■ Need for self-determination

Each person within the family has an innate urge to become independent and to be seen for her own unique self. This is the basis of high self-esteem. Within many families this need for one's own distinct identity is not valued and respected. Partners try to control, manipulate and coerce each other into being what they want each other to be. Equally, parents can project their problems and dependencies onto children and force children along paths that suit the parents rather than the children. When parents see children as extensions of themselves they may want their children to be clever, beautiful, successful, artistic, musical, athletic and so on. Many children yield to these pressures from parents but they are bound to rebel inwardly, as do adults and adolescents. As children and adolescents become more powerful and competent they need to be given a greater role in making decisions about their own lives. I have helped a great number of adults who, when they came for help, were living their lives for their parents and not pursuing their own destinies. Therapy involved helping them to separate out from their parents' projections onto them and to establish their own unique pathways in life.

There are three main aspects to helping family members become self-determined:

- Accept the family member as she is. Each person needs to be recognised for her own unique skills, abilities and unique ways of perceiving the world
- Encourage each family member to pursue interests and increase skills that are special to her
- Allow each family member the freedom to choose what she does best, and provide the support and if possible the material resources necessary

■ Need for freedom

Without freedom, family members cannot learn to become self-sufficient. Freedom enables the exploration of new areas of knowledge, new friendships, new skills, different recreational pursuits and educational options. Most of all, freedom allows for the development of a sense of responsibility. Indeed, freedom and responsibility go hand in hand. The more responsibility children show, the more freedom they need to be given. When freedom is not used responsibly, privileges need to be withdrawn for a period of time. However, another opportunity for exercising freedom has to be provided as otherwise the desired responsible behaviour cannot be learned. Of course, it is equally important that couples allow each other the freedom to pursue individual interests, hobbies, friendships, spiritual paths, careers and so on. In troubled couple relationships this freedom is blocked frequently, thereby adding further to the conflict.

Unfortunately, because of the risks involved, many parents hesitate to give their children the freedom they need in order to become responsible and able. This is an unwise practice as over-protection leads to helplessness, an inability to be responsible for oneself and chronic dependence on others. The following guidelines may help in this regard:

- The more responsibility shown, the more freedom you give
- When you grant freedom, evaluate how it is used: Is the child reliable and suitably cautious? Does he employ the freedom well to get the task done or meet a challenge? Is a serious effort made? How well does the child follow through on commitments?

It is very important that when freedom is allowed the limits and conditions are stated clearly and specifically:

- 'Yes, you can go and play in your friend's house but I want you home here at 6.00 p.m.'
- 'Yes, you can play football but I don't want you playing football on the road.'
- 'Yes, you can go to the disco but there must be no alcohol and you must be home at 1.00 a.m.'

When you are clear and specific, it is much easier to evaluate whether the child has met the commitments laid down. Explain to children that by making commitments and following them through, they demonstrate how trustworthy they are and that this leads to extra freedom. Like many adults, children will attempt to slide out of commitments and will want the freedom but not the responsibilities that go with it. They may complain bitterly when they cannot get their own way as a ploy to make you feel guilty. If you yield to such manipulation, you are likely to regret it as eventually the child will get into trouble. Be positively firm; firmness and love go hand in hand.

■ Need for self-confidence

Many people confuse confidence with competence. They believe that if you are good at doing something you will feel confident. This is not necessarily true. There are many people who are highly skilled but are utterly devoid of confidence. Self-confidence needs to be present *before* competence. People who lack confidence, in spite of evident competence, perpetually fear failure, rejection or disaster and are rarely at peace within themselves.

Confidence is the conviction that you have all the resources necessary to understand, cope with and survive in your world. This conviction is fostered by parents who model such self-confidence and who also frequently affirm their children's limitless potential for learning. When you see children (or adults) trying to achieve something, let them know how pleased you are to see them making such efforts and encourage them that, once they persist, they can achieve what they are aiming for. The emphasis must be on effort, not performance. Emphasis on performance may lead to avoidance, compensation, rebelliousness or apathy. Encouragement of effort and affirmation of the person's limitless capacity are the foundations for building self-confidence and competence.

■ Need for a sense of humour

A sense of humour keeps us close to reality. Once it is of a healthy, non-hostile nature, humour helps family members to view problems, uncertainties and fears in a not over-serious way. Good humour shows that each of us is fallible. Laughing at our mistakes, omissions, slips of tongue and failures softens the impact of such experiences and sets the positive ground for learning from mistakes and failures. Here again, it is important that parents model a light-hearted response to their own difficulties, inconsistencies, delusions of grandeur, snobbishness and pompousness. When children witness this they will learn not to take life so seriously and to laugh at their own inconsistencies and frailties.

❑ *Needs of the couple*

It is not too difficult to catalogue the needs that arise in a couple relationship.

Checklist of needs of the couple
• The need for love and security
• The need for care and support
• The need to offer love, security, care and support to others
• The need for sexual gratification
• The need for parenthood
• The need to share responsibilities of rearing children
• The need for direct and clear communication
• The need for social outings
• The need for financial equality and security
• The need for educational and/or occupational progress
• The need for personal independence

The problem in couple relationships can be that each partner has a different definition of each of these needs. The kind of giving and receiving that occurs in meeting needs is dependent on each partner's own particular definitions of these needs, definitions which are part and parcel of each person's own definition of themselves.

It is as if we live to answer the question: 'who am I?' In your relationship with your partner the activities you undertake to meet the other's needs are employed subconsciously to answer this question and validate the answer you wish to adopt. When a person is insecure, has a dislike or hate of self, doubts her physical and sexual attractiveness or believes she is socially inadequate, then the meeting of a partner's needs and the expression of her own needs become fraught with misinterpretation, intolerance and hypersensitivity to criticism and rejection. Unless each of the partners resolves their hidden self-esteem problems it is highly unlikely that their relationship will be positively and reciprocally constructed for the benefit of each other.

It is important that each partner in the couple is aware of the other's needs and that they do their best to create a supportive, loving and active relationship wherein those needs are met.

■ The need for love and security

Unconditional acceptance and love of each other fulfil this need for love and security. Unconditional regard means not only that the partner is loved for herself and not for what she does but also that no matter what happens in terms of unacceptable behaviour, she is secure that love and acceptance will not be withdrawn. Of course, the inappropriate behaviour is not tolerated but it is treated as separate from the person. Regular demonstrations of affection, surprise gifts and outings, appreciation of each other and strong interest in each other's lives all help in meeting the need for love and security.

■ The need for care and support

When a couple relationship is constructed for the mutual care and support of each other, it is much easier for the partners to cope with any personal, interpersonal, career or other difficulties that may arise. There are many couples where the partners do not give each other this care and support in times of crisis or even in the day-to-day stresses of running a home. These partners are riddled with personal insecurities and are not able to support and care for themselves not to mind support and care for each other. But, with guidance, any couple can develop a supportive atmosphere wherein both partners can begin to increase their own sense of self and gradually begin to exhibit greater caring and support of each other.

■ The need to offer love, security, care and support to others

In secure couple relationships, each partner is given the freedom to offer love, security, care and support to others – whether to children, parents, brothers or sisters, other relatives, friends, neighbours or colleagues. In insecure couple relationships such reaching out to others threatens the insecure, vulnerable partner and becomes a source of conflict within the relationship. It is important that the giving to others outside the couple relationship is balanced by a giving within the relationship; otherwise a partner may be justified in the complaint that 'you're always there for others, but never for me'. Over-giving to others is yet another sign of dependence and low self-esteem. Charity begins at home: with yourself, with your partner and with your children.

■ The need for sexual gratification

In harmonious couple relationships the expression and fulfilment of sexual needs are given due priority. Where there are unresolved intimacy issues, these often find expression in and interfere with the meeting of sexual needs. Research has shown that 60 per cent of psychosexual problems are due to underlying marital difficulties and the self-esteem difficulties of each of the partners. Resolving these issues is necessary before sexual problems can be tackled and very often when they are resolved the sexual difficulties disappear.

The couple relationship can become the ideal situation wherein both partners feel good about their bodies, their sexual urges, the expression of these urges and the mutual pleasuring of each other. Whilst an active sexual life between partners is not sufficient in itself to maintain a couple relationship it certainly is a considerable bonus.

■ The need for parenthood

Parenthood is an important need for some partners and this is something which should be discussed before entering a commitment to each other. Parenting is a huge responsibility and not one to be undertaken lightly. It has been considered in detail in Chapter 1.

■ The need to share responsibilities of rearing children

When there is a couple decision to parent children, then there equally needs to be a couple commitment to share the responsibilities that result from that decision. Even though attitudes are changing, women up to now largely have been loaded with the task of rearing children. Some women block men (who allow it of course!) from being involved with the children. These women are generally living their lives through their children and the father, in such cases, needs to be assertive in establishing his right to joint parenting. Neither can he turn a blind eye to his wife's overprotection of the children. However, this attitude is all too common and the effects can be devastating.

There are many tasks involved in rearing children and joint parenting clearly leads to less stress. Examples of such tasks are:

- Feeding the children
- Bathing the children
- Disciplining the children
- Watching over the children
- Playing with the children
- Talking to the children
- Reading to the children
- Helping the children when needed
- Helping with school homework
- Providing relief from parenting

■ The need for direct and clear communication

Communication difficulties are the most common sign of couple and family problems. Silences, aggression, manipulation, withdrawal, non-expression of needs or feelings – all affect the well-being of the partners and their relationship. Direct and clear communication is essential to the fulfilment of couple needs. The whole area of communication is dealt with in considerable detail in Chapter 8.

■ The need for social outings

'You never take me out' is a common complaint in unhappy couple relationships. The more a couple are involved together socially, the greater the level of intimacy, friendship and companionship. There are many activities that a couple can do together:

- Go to the cinema/theatre/bowling alley/nightclub/pub
- Go shopping
- Have a meal out
- Attend parties, celebrations
- Go on walks
- Participate in a sporting activity (for example, tennis, fishing, squash, golf)
- Go and watch a sporting activity
- Have friends over for a meal
- Have a night in alone
- Take a weekend break
- Have a holiday alone
- Do a night course/attend a lecture/talk/seminar

It is important that partners let each other know what their social needs are and not wait for one another to read each other's mind. Remember you have a right to ask; asking does not mean you will get all your needs met but it does mean you are owning and taking responsibility for them. When important social needs are consistently not being met by your partner then confrontation becomes necessary.

■ The need for financial equality and security

Money can be quite a contentious issue even in the best of relationships and in the worst of relationships it can become a major stick with which the partners beat each other. It is wise that partners maintain financial independence and that income is divided between family requirements and the partners' personal requirements. When both partners have their own personal allowance it is up to each to decide what they want to do with it and neither of them has to account to the other for it. Some husbands can be worse than accountants in looking for detailed evidence of expenditure. This is one way for a man who is insecure to wield power by increasing his partner's dependence on him and reducing the threat of her leaving him.

Discussion and negotiation are needed in the allocation of money for family expenditure on such items as mortgage, heating, food, savings and buying presents. What is important is that the relationship with your partner is not jeopardised over money matters, and that differences which arise are ironed out in the context of a supportive and caring environment. When there is a risk of one partner becoming aggressive, it is best to leave the issue and return to it later when both people are calmer.

■ The need for educational and/or occupational progress

Balance is the operative word in the context of the need for educational and/or occupational progress. Men are notorious for spending too much time at their jobs with the consequent neglect of other need areas within the couple relationship and the family. They also still tend to think that their careers are more important than those of their female partners but this is a recipe for conflict. A partner's job can have either positive or detrimental effects. When the job is suitably located, when there is a good degree of job satisfaction, when the salary provides a good income, when it provides pleasurable social opportunities, then its effects are likely to be positive on the couple relationship. However, if the job requires long-distance travel or a lot of time away from home, if it is stressful or un-fulfilling, if it pays poorly, or if it demands long hours, then its effects can be detrimental to the couple relationship.

The main issue here is that there needs to be mutual interest, support, encouragement and allocation of resources (time and money) for the career and educational development of each partner. More and more, continuing education is becoming necessary to keep abreast of the demands of employers and the social, cultural and technological changes that are occurring.

■ The need for personal independence

When two people live together they must not lose sight of their own unique identity and must maintain a level of independence. If a couple 'live in each other's pocket' they can suffocate one another and block individual development. The couple relationship needs to be open to facilitate not only the partnership between them but also the independent life of each one. Many couple relationships have faltered on the romantic myth which says 'we must do everything together'. Partners need to make it easy for each other to have:

- A night out by oneself
- A day off for oneself
- The right to drive the car by oneself
- Money easily available without having to ask one's partner
- The right to make household decisions without always having to ask one's partner
- Freedom to go to social and other events without one's partner
- The right to invite one's own friends in to the home

❏ *Needs of the family*

When the needs of the individual members and of the couple are being met there are still family needs to be considered in creating a happy family life.

Checklist of needs of the family
• The need for an atmosphere of unconditional love, support, caring and understanding
• The need for physical nurturance
• The need for order, harmony and maintenance of the family unit
• The need for safety to express needs and feelings
• The need for family get-togethers inside the home
• The need for social outings
• The need to share household responsibilities
• The need for spirituality

■ The need for an atmosphere of unconditional love

This need has been considered in detail in Chapter 4. Suffice to reiterate here that how family members relate to each other is the mirror of the level of well-being of that family. You can sense the atmosphere when you go into many homes: tense, serious, strained, humorous, caring, formal, informal, competitive. By offering unconditional loving, caring, support and understanding of one another, family members can give each other a home that is a pleasure to be in, to return to and to which to bring one's friends. When relationships are enmeshed or neglectful, then the atmosphere is such that very often family members become lost to the home either by being frequently physically absent or by retreating into the safety of avoidance of contact.

■ The need for physical nurturance

Physical nurturance refers to the basic needs of a family for food, clothing, heat, housing, money and so on. In a caring family, such needs are catered for as best as can be done within the social circumstances of the family (for example, employment status, family size). In neglectful families, resources may be wasted on gambling, alcohol, spending sprees, overindulgent activities or drug taking. When basic physical needs are not being met within a family, emotional and social needs are likely to be neglected.

■ The need for order, harmony and maintenance of the family unit

This primarily involves leadership, where parents attempt to ensure that order, harmony and regular family contact are maintained and that when problems occur immediate efforts are made to resolve them. It also entails the maintenance of family boundaries so that outsiders (in-laws, other relatives, friends, neighbours) are not allowed to interfere with family life. I have worked with many families where, because parents could not say 'no' to others, outsiders were allowed to have an undue negative influence on family life.

■ The need for safety

Clearly a family needs to feel physically safe from violence and assault from both within and outside the family. Violence is always a non-negotiable issue and must not be tolerated from any source. Equally important as safety from violence is the safety of being able to express all of one's feelings and needs without fear or repercussion – physical or otherwise. Too often, family members suppress, repress or deny their feelings or blame them on others, resulting in considerable family disharmony. The clear message within the family needs to be that it is safe to bring up any issue and that caring consideration will be given to any positively expressed needs and feelings. (The way feelings are best expressed and responded to is covered in Chapter 7.)

■ The need for family get-togethers

Family morale is very much linked to the amount of contact that occurs between family members. Some families interact like ships that pass in the night but never make contact. Of course, when they collide the damage caused can be great. The more family members positively interact with each other, the greater is the sense of family. Certainly, meal times and some recreation times are ideal opportunities for all members to get together as a family. It is also a good idea to have regular family meetings (say, once weekly) to give each other the opportunity to voice issues. These meetings can be an occasion for repeating the values, expectations and responsibilities that are crucial to family harmony. Problem-solving meetings are also important as are planning meetings with regard to, for example, holidays, budgeting, care for a member who is not well, career and educational pursuits. All family members (even the baby) need to be present at the meetings. Children quickly sense when they are an integral part of the family and when they have only 'second-class citizenship'.

■ The need for social outings

Research into the lives of troubled children and adolescents has indicated that often they are members of a family who rarely, if ever, go out socially together. Children often boast about the holidays they have with their parents, the football matches attended together, the film, the pantomime, the museum, the school play seen together. Very often parents assume that adolescents do not want to be seen out with them. The opposite is true, but parents need to be sensitive to the way they relate to adolescents when out socially; treat them like children and they become embarrassed and annoyed. Giving adolescents the freedom to be with their own friends makes it even more likely that family get-togethers remain important to them. It is important to include children and adolescents when choices are being made about social and holiday excursions.

■ **The need to share household responsibilities**

The sharing of household responsibilities can be a considerable bone of contention within some families. The key issue here is that maintaining the home is the responsibility of all family members, not just Mum or Dad. The earlier children are given domestic responsibilities the better. Problems often occur when children who were used to having no demands made of them are suddenly presented with household tasks. It entails considerable consistency and firmness to correct earlier neglect of training children for domestic responsibilities. Traditionally, fathers have got away with believing that the home was the domain of the mother and that they did not have to have hand, act or part in the everyday home responsibilities. It is difficult for children to accept one law for them and another for their father. Fathers need to act as models for children and firmly encourage them to do their share within the home. Efforts of all family members must be praised and, occasionally, tangibly rewarded. Parents must not slip into the response of 'it's easier and quicker if I do it myself'. When that happens others are allowed to avoid what is equally their responsibility. When there is fair sharing of household tasks there is far less scope for resentment and feelings of 'being put upon' by anyone in the family.

■ **The need for spirituality**

There are many paths to developing a sense of spirituality. Different religions are examples of different searches for meaning. There is no right or wrong path; each family and, later on as an adult, each individual family member needs to find their own meaning to life and the universe. Building self-esteem appears to be an essential aspect of developing spirituality. It is interesting that the psychologist Abraham Maslow lists frequent mystical experiences as an indicator of self-actualisation. One of my favourite authors, Bernie Siegel, claims that he is a mystic because he is a surgeon; he says that he sees the body heal itself in ways that medicine is not even remotely close to achieving. Psalm 8 of the Old Testament says 'Thank you Lord for the wonder of my being'. Helping family members to attain a sense of their wonder as unique persons, with wondrous capacities, living in a world of unique individuals and beauty, supports the process of finding a spiritual dimension to life. Fostering the use of intuition (the unconscious wisdom that is available to us) is a good family practice. Developing a sense of the wonder of the universe is also helped by meditation, prayer, relaxation, love of others and the love of life. Encouragement of silence, peace and retreat from an overactive world can also lead to 'mystical' experiences. I recall that once following some university examinations I retreated to a remote mountainy area where I experienced a feeling of transcendence and a great sense of universal meaning. I wrote this verse in an attempt to capture those precious moments.

Something Else

On a moon-lit rock man
gazing at the heavens
a cat angled
its way to my feet
met with defeat;
a stroke of affection
would have made a friend
but a different kind
of peace had captured me,
I let the cat go free.

❏ *Confrontation on unmet needs*

In many families a blind eye is turned when one member witnesses another member (whether parent or child) being rejected or abused. Outsiders (relatives, neighbours, friends or teachers) may also be aware of such neglect. Outsiders often rationalise that it is not their place to interfere. There may be some grounds for such a rationalisation in the case of adults but, where children are concerned, no excuse is strong enough for failure to act. I have worked with families where one of the parents or an adult outsider witnessed children being hurt, humiliated and physically or even sexually abused but nothing was done. So many times unmet needs of family members go unconfronted under the banner of 'for peace sake' or the cause of not upsetting the father or mother. The reason for inaction on the part of an adult family member or an outsider almost always relates to the witness's own poor self-esteem.

The problem is that the whole family loses out when neglected needs are not confronted. Clearly, the parent who mistreats her own child or partner is in need of professional help and failure to confront the mistreatment leads to perpetuation or even worsening of that parent's problems. On the other hand, the family members who are the victims of such abuse develop severe self-esteem difficulties due to feeling unloved, unwanted and not feeling good enough. When children are involved, they learn to imitate the neglectful behaviours of the parent who is abusive and the whole cycle is likely to repeat itself in their own lives and later on in the lives of their families. No change is now possible and the sad process of gross emotional neglect or conditional loving or physical or sexual abuse continues, setting up obstacles to the mature development of each member of the family.

Confrontation is not blaming; if it takes the form of judging and blaming it leads to an exacerbation of the neglect being addressed. Confrontation is an act of caring, a caring as much for the perpetrator as for the victim of the neglect. It involves the direct and clear expression by a member of the family of some unmet need. It must not be an attack on the other family member, as an attack assumes that the perpetrator is being deliberately neglectful. This is not only a major assumption but it is also a judgment and a criticism and will lead to a strong defensive action on the part of the family member attacked. Family members do not intentionally hurt and neglect each other but, in order to protect themselves from possible rejection, they subconsciously resort to a range of behaviours that lead, unfortunately, to other family members being ignored, dismissed, abused, judged, criticised or scolded. The following examples clarify the process.

Take an adolescent boy who has been regularly dominated, controlled, negatively labelled and criticised by his father. This boy is blocked by his father from meeting his needs to be reasonably free, to be different, to make his own friends, to determine his own educational goals, to decide on his own career path and to carry out tasks in his own unique way. But the father's 'blocking' behaviours are not there to prevent his son from developing his own identity and life-path but rather serve as an insurance against the boy not needing him. This father has very low self-esteem and subconsciously believes that he is not worthy in his own right to impress his son and can only do so by means of always being right. Similarly, the mother who passively accepts abuse of herself and her children by her husband is not deliberately neglecting herself and her children. She has neither the belief in herself nor the independence to be able to counter her husband's behaviour and hopes that by acquiescing she will gain acceptance and protection from further hurt and rejection. This mother would need much support in order to confront her husband's neglectful actions.

For adult members of a family the first step in confrontation is verbal and involves:

- Direct communication (using the name of the family member involved)
- An 'I' message
- Declaration of how you feel
- Expression of your needs

This kind of verbal confrontation is very often all that is needed but there are times when the other person does not respond and a further step – active confrontation – is then required.

Using these guidelines, in the example given above, the woman who is passive might verbally assert: 'John, when you shout and roar at me and the children, I feel terrified and I need you to communicate calmly and positively to me and the children.' This message may not be well received by the father who is aggressive and dominating, and may lead to an increase in his attempts to control his wife and children. The reason for this is that confrontation serves to weaken the protective weapon of the husband and, initially, he is likely to wield it all the more in the hope of regaining power. In this case the wife needs to go beyond the verbal confrontation to the level of active confrontation. The actions needed in this woman's situation include not responding to the aggressive expression of needs by her husband; warning him that if abuse of herself and the children continues she will seek outside help; and if that does not get the desired response, then acting on that resolve.

It is important not to threaten an action unless you fully intend to follow it through. So much confrontation is unproductive because family members do not follow through on the actions that are necessary to ensure that caring responses are created within the family. There have been men who have threatened me because I supported their wives in getting a protection order. I point out to them that the protection order is not against them but has the purpose of protecting their wives and children from abuse and of upholding their right to a peaceful and loving home atmosphere. I further point out that when they are ready to respond positively to the needs of their wives and children, there will no longer be a need for the protection order.

Confrontation can be a creative force within the family and its absence leads to a spiralling of problems. A valuable practice for families is to have a weekly forum where each family member can air any grievances and express any unmet needs or fears, dreams and wishes. Parents can take the lead here by letting each other and the children know what their reasonable expectations are and by encouraging the other family members to express their needs. Apart from the weekly forum, permission to voice unmet needs must be regularly repeated and reinforced.

Children are in a much weaker position when it comes to confrontation and often have to depend on adults to take up their cause for them. However, they are frequently let down in this regard. Children are always victims but they do not see this; usually they blame themselves for their parents' neglectful behaviours and label themselves as 'bad', 'stupid', 'no good', 'ugly', 'lazy', 'unlovable' and so on. It has already been pointed out that, though parents are not to blame for the neglect they perpetrate on children, they are responsible for the consequences of their behaviours and need to firmly resolve to undo what harm they have done. If they refuse to take responsibility, then strong action is needed on the part of adults outside the family to ensure that neglect is not perpetuated. My own experience is that parents respond positively to sensitive and caring but firm confrontation. Those who resist have been badly damaged themselves and even stronger action is needed to protect children from these parents, who are in great need of help themselves.

Chapter 7

Making the Most of Feelings within the Family

❏ *All feelings are positive!*
- Welfare feelings
- Emergency feelings
- Feelings cannot hurt another!

❏ *Expressing feelings*
- Your feelings are about yourself
- Non-expression of feelings
- Open expression of feelings
  - ➯ **Expressing welfare feelings**
  - ➯ **Expressing emergency feelings**

❏ *Responding to feelings*
- The other person's feelings are not about you
- Importance of responsiveness to feelings
- Positive responding to another's feelings

A tip-off to an abusive family system is a situation in which nobody ever apologises.
Karen Shaud

❏ *All feelings are positive!*

Western culture has done a great disservice to healthy human development by viewing certain emotions as positive and others as negative. Typically, feelings such as love, confidence, joy, enthusiasm and optimism are seen as 'good' and 'positive' while feelings such as fear, anger, depression, guilt and resentment are viewed as 'bad' and 'negative'. It is not surprising then that many people have difficulties in expressing the so-called negative emotions. In many ways the major caring professions conspire to suppress, explain away or medicalise 'negative' feelings. For example, there are prescribed drugs available for the three most common feelings of all – fear, anger and depression;

113

there is no readily available forum for children or teachers to express their feelings within educational settings and the same is true of workplaces. What happens in each of these systems is unfortunately prefigured in the family.

A further crime that is daily committed against human emotions arises from the stereotyping of males and females. Men fare worse in this instance as the stereotype leaves them emotionally illiterate; not only is it not permissible for the man to express such feelings as fear, sadness or vulnerability but it is also seen as 'sissyish' to reveal love, tenderness or gentleness. Women, on the other hand, are allowed more expression of the 'positive' feelings and it is quite acceptable for them to reveal fear but they suffer severe difficulties in expressing anger or depression. While anger is 'allowed' for men, regrettably they often express it aggressively.

Contrary to these depictions, I believe that all feelings are positive. Emotions are never wrong and are the surest indicators of the person's internal state at any one moment. So, rather than use the terms positive and negative, I prefer to describe the 'good' feelings as welfare feelings and the 'bad' feelings as emergency feelings. Parents act as models for their children and how the parents deal with feelings largely determines the levels of emotional expression and responsiveness within the family.

■ Welfare feelings

Welfare feelings are well titled since when you feel relaxed, calm, confident, contented, happy, joyful, secure, loving or compassionate, you are in a welfare state. Welfare feelings reveal to you that what you are presently doing is positive and productive. The expression of these feelings needs to be greeted with similar feelings of joy, delight and caring so that the person expressing them is affirmed in his welfare state of mind and body.

■ Emergency feelings

Feelings like anger, sadness, depression, guilt, resentment and jealousy all signal that there is an emotional emergency –

whether within yourself or between yourself and another – which needs resolution. These feelings act as an 'alarm' trying to wake you up to the need for some internal or external action. It is with these feelings that many families have difficulties. However, these families are missing the enormous positive benefits to be gained from these feelings. Not many would dispute the fact that pain is positive as it alerts you to the need for physical healing. In the same way, emergency emotions alert you to the need for emotional healing. For example, when you experience anger in your relationship with another, that anger is letting you know that there is some need of yours not being met in the relationship and it is providing you with the energy to express your need. How, though, is depression positive? Again, this feeling either alerts you to a serious emotional problem within yourself or indicates difficulty adjusting to some loss experience (for example, death of spouse, loss of status, breakdown of a relationship). Depression in my own life eventually alerted me to a hate of myself and the need to correct my relationship with myself. When a child is fearful this emotion is there to alert parents (or other adults) to some aspect of life with which the child is not coping and with which she needs help. No matter what the emergency feeling is, it always has a message that some change is needed. These feelings are the most vital barometer of the family's everyday emotional well-being.

■ Feelings cannot hurt another!

One of the reasons most frequently given for not revealing certain emergency feelings is: 'I'm afraid of hurting the other person.' The danger, however, is that if you do not express these feelings, you may very well end up hurting another. It is important to realise that feelings cannot hurt anyone but actions can. The way you express your feelings is a vital issue as an inappropriate communication of feelings can leave the other person feeling devastated. Many people express anger aggressively; however it is not the anger that hurts the receiver but the aggression in its expression. If when you are angry you storm at your partner shouting 'you're a miserable, selfish bitch', it is the 'put-down' aggressive message that damages your partner's self-image. The original anger in this case is lost in a sea of aggression and it is very unlikely that your unmet need will be addressed. If, on the other hand, you own your feeling of anger as a revelation about yourself and express it in a way that is respectful of yourself and the other person, the emergency issue giving rise to the anger may be resolved. If, for example, the underlying issue had to do with decision-making, the appropriate communication might be something like: 'I have difficulty when decisions are made about the children's schooling and I am not consulted. I'm asking that in future I be included in such decision-making.'

A situation that often arises is where one person in a relationship has lost interest in the relationship and is afraid of letting the other person know of this emotional development because of fears that the other person will not cope with the revelation. I have encountered couples who, because of such fears, went ahead and married each other even though they had serious doubts about the durability of the relationship. It is a misconceived protection not to let the other person know your true feelings, particularly when it concerns the relationship. There is also the hidden issue of your own fear of not being able to cope with the other person's possible emotional reaction to the revelation; the protection in this case extends beyond the other to yourself.

Sometimes members of a family may not reveal troublesome feelings because of not wanting to burden others with their problems. It is important to remember that letting your partner know how you feel is not saying 'take responsibility for me'; it is simply asking for support and perhaps advice. The responsibility for the called-for action remains with you. In the case of a child who does not want to burden parents, the problem lies with the parents whom the child intuitively picks up as being unable to cope with the expression of certain feelings. The child now becomes protective of the parents and the emergency issue goes unresolved. The parents are responsible but, due to their own vulnerability, they are not exercising this responsibility.

❏ *Expressing feelings*

▪ Your feelings are about yourself

One of the more important lessons children need to learn is that their feelings are always about themselves – revelations of their needs, for example, to be loved, affirmed, held, listened to, or praised. Unfortunately, most parents do not realise that their own feelings are about themselves and so cannot teach this essential lesson to their children. Parents tend to blame either each other or the children for how they themselves feel. Often parents 'suffer in silence'. In other words, rather than seeing feelings as being about themselves, they see them as saying something about the other. Nothing is further from the

Communications where sender blames another for own feelings	
Children to parents	'You made me cry.' 'You don't love me.' 'You hate me.' 'You love Mary more than you love me.' 'You made me sad.' 'You hurt me.'
Parent to parent	'You're the one who makes me miserable.' 'You're impossible to live with.' 'You depress me.' 'You're always out.' 'You don't love me anymore.' 'Did you think of me all day?' 'You only think about yourself.' 'Your family are more important than me.'
Parents to children	'You're driving me mad.' 'You're a bad boy.' 'You're useless.' 'You're a selfish little girl.' 'You're a noisy brat.' 'You're bold.' 'You're naughty.' 'You're stupid.'

truth. The feeling is in you and must therefore be about you; to begin to own and take responsibility for your feelings you need to grasp this fundamental reality. Blaming another for your feelings typically leads to hurt, anger or withdrawal on the other person's part and does nothing to resolve your unmet needs.

When you examine these examples of communication you will notice that there is not one word about the person sending the message in the words spoken. Furthermore, because the messages blame the other, he will either retaliate or withdraw and the hidden unmet need of the sender goes unspoken. If, however, the sender owns his own feelings, the communication involved takes on a completely different form.

Communications where sender owns own feelings

Children to parents	'I'm crying because I don't feel you love me.'
	'I am worried that you don't love me.'
	'I feel rejected.'
	'I am frightened that you may love Mary more than you love me.'
	'I'm sad that you do not want to play with me.'
	'I don't want you to hold me so tight as it hurts me.'
Parent to parent	'I feel miserable and lonely when you choose to go out every night.'
	'I'm unhappy and unfulfilled in our relationship.'
	'I do find it depressing when you are constantly critical of me and I need to be shown more regard and appreciation.'
	'I am unhappy when I'm alone here in the evenings and would like more time with you.'
	'I am deeply worried that you no longer feel anything for me.'
	'I do wish that at times you would think of me during the day.' →

'I do need you to show me more love and affection.'

'I often feel rejected when you put your mother's needs before mine.'

Parents to children	'John and Mary, I can't cope with the noise you're making any longer and I need you to play more quietly.'
	'Michael, I feel angry when you hit your sister and I do not want to see it happen again.'
	'I am disappointed with your effort to clean up the sitting room and I'm requesting you to finish what has been left undone.'
	'I would like you to share the sweets I gave you with your brother.'
	'Eddie, I've got a headache right now and I need you to play more quietly.'
	'I am angry that you did not do as I requested.'
	'Mary, I did not like you going to my purse without permission.'
	'I am dissatisfied with your homework exercise and I believe you can make a greater effort.'

When parents own their own feelings, interpret them accurately as being about themselves and communicate them in a way that demonstrates ownership, children will imitate them. However, the converse is also true; when parents either bottle up feelings or blame them on other family members, children will tend to repeat the same process. Such a family will experience much hurt, anger and alienation.

■ Non-expression of feelings

Because feelings are the most accurate and powerful indicators of what is going on in a person's life, any level of silence around feelings can have devastating effects on a family's emotional, social and physical well-being. When family members cannot express welfare feelings to each other, deep insecurity regarding being loved will abide. Very often the children of these families where love is unexpressed find it extremely difficult to form any close and intimate relationships as adults; avoidance becomes very strong as the risk of rejection is overwhelming and it is safer not to express one's emotional needs.

The non-expression of emergency feelings is more common within families that are distressed. Because of stereotyping, many women do not express feelings of anger or dissatisfaction as this would run contrary to the social ideals set for them. The children who identify with such a mother will develop similar emotional reticence. Conversely, children who identify with fathers who express anger in aggressive ways, or who deny feelings of fear, upset, vulnerability or sadness or who have difficulty in expressing welfare feelings will repeat the pattern of this male parent. This suppression of feelings by both the parents and the children means that many essential needs within the family never reach the surface.

Suppression refers to the situation where you know you are bottling up your feelings for fear of what others might say or how others might react. *Repression* is a far more serious matter as in this case you are not consciously aware of cutting off your own feelings. The following experiences of a client of mine illustrate the powerful effect of repression of feelings in childhood.

This young woman was sent to me by her general practitioner for a persistent pain in her side for which he could find no organic basis. She refused to go into hospital for any tests as she had a severe phobia of hospitals. She also, curiously, presented with a phobia of appendicitis. When she came for the first session, she told me the pain was persistent but could vary from mild to severe and was situated deep down on her right side. She was now twenty-five years of age. She felt the pain was there for a very long time and, eventually, we traced its beginnings to age two-and-a-half to three years. During the session she told me that a long-term relationship she had been having with a man had suddenly come to an end. What was curious in the recounting of this traumatic experience was that she kept smiling at me. I now asked myself a number of questions:

- What was this young woman doing with this pain for twenty-two years?
- What had led to her having a fixed smile on her face?
- What was the protective function of the phobia of appendicitis?
- What was the protective function of the phobia of hospitals?

I actually knew both her parents and neither of them could cope with any expression of emotional upset. When this woman was a young child, like other children, she would have cried, got angry and been frightened, upset and frustrated. However, on display of these feelings her parents would have got anxious and been unable to cope. When parents cannot cope, a child's security is hugely threatened. Because the child is highly dependent on parents and believes she cannot exist without them, she will subconsciously resort to a behaviour that will keep her parents healthy and coping. The young woman with the pain learned that 'if I keep smiling up at Mummy and Daddy and hide my feelings of upset, fear, anger, etc. then they will not get upset'. There is now medical evidence that adults who go around with a permanent smile on their faces and have an inability to express hostile feelings are prone to cancer. It is as if the buried resentment, sadness, anger and hostility converts into a physical cancer. People often speak of buried anger and resentment as 'being like a cancer eating you up inside'.

But why did the child develop the pain in her side? The physical pain got her some attention but it also represented the deeper emotional pain and strain she could not express. The phobia of appendicitis had to do with her fear that this pain might ever be taken away because should this happen, the deeper emotional pain would never have a chance of being discovered. The phobia of hospitals was even more revealing; this again had to do with the fear of the pain being explained away, but there was another factor. In hospitals many patients are terrified, depressed, frightened, lonely, sad, resentful and angry: how could she face into such emotions when she had learned to repress them for over twenty years? Indeed, she had become vulnerable like her parents, unable to cope with emergency feelings. If she found herself in a hospital, the likelihood was that she would have a breakdown, flooded by all the upset of other patients. Of course, if she broke down the danger was that her parents would in turn cease to cope. Treatment for this young woman entailed helping her to begin to express all her emergency feelings.

Denial of feelings is common among people with addiction problems (alcohol, food, drugs). It can also occur when people are told that they have a serious illness, or when a loved one dies or when people are given bad news about a son or daughter. How many parents have responded to bad news with 'my child would never do anything like you are suggesting'? Denial is a protection against threats to self-esteem; as long as you blind yourself to the issue you do not have to look at and face up to the reality of your own vulnerability.

The most common maladaptive way of expressing feelings is to blame others for what you are experiencing. This may be aggressive or passive-aggressive – hostile silences, physical and emotional withdrawal or withholding of privileges. When blamed, the other person will feel put upon, manipulated or abused and is likely to either attack back or withdraw to protect himself. Remember you are entirely responsible for your own feelings and it is up to you to own them and express them in constructive ways.

One of the regular complaints I hear in couple therapy is that 'he never shows me any feeling'. Another typical complaint is 'I never know what he's feeling'. When parents do not express welfare feelings to each other, deep in-security develops in their relationship. Genuine demonstration – both verbal and non-verbal – of love, concern, gentleness, tenderness, warmth, joy and confidence in one another needs to be a regular feature of the couple relationship. Such expression of welfare feelings deepens the couple relationship, makes it more secure and enhances the self-esteem of each partner. An added bonus is that it also increases the security of the children of the couple as the welfare of their parents' relationship is important to their mature development.

When parents do not demonstrate welfare feelings to their children, the door to their emotional development begins to close. More than anything else children need to know they are loved and on this issue there is no such thing as benign neglect. The absence of welfare feelings in the home provides only an arid ground from which no healthy growth can occur. I have worked with children from such loveless homes who hide their feelings of unlovability behind masks of aggression, delinquency, fantasy and destructiveness or behind absorption in instrumental activities where no relationships are involved and where therefore there is no rejection risk. Some of these children spend most of their time out of the home and try to find recognition in the homes of peers. I recall one child who, from the age of four years, used to knock at the door of a local orphanage asking to be let in because he perceived the orphanage as more loving than his home.

When care workers went to the orphanages in Romania and walked down the corridors of cots of emotionally neglected children, they found that the children just lay still, not expecting anyone to show them love. After some weeks of nurturing, embracing, playing and loving, the hands of the children reached up for affection when the care workers walked down the corridors. The emotional breakthrough to older orphans took a lot more time than with the younger children. They had been starved of love too long to risk responding prematurely to a change in adults' behaviour. Sadly, some parents who adopted older orphans found them so unresponsive to their expressions of welfare feelings that they felt like giving the orphans back. But once love continues to be shown unconditionally, children will eventually find the safety to respond. To 'give them back' would only copperfasten these children's conviction that they are unlovable. When you give love, only give to give; when you give to get you are showing your own dependence and, unwittingly, you are attempting to manipulate loving responses from others. Children are intuitive, particularly those who are vulnerable, and they will strongly resist such attempts at manipulation.

■ Open expression of feelings

A characteristic of the healthy family is the open expression of all feelings. Parents need to take the lead here. Ownership of the feeling experienced is a prerequisite to its honest, genuine and caring expression.

⮢ Expressing welfare feelings

For many people expressing welfare feelings comes easier than expressing emergency emotions. Many adults feel safe in expressing welfare feelings to children but show greater reticence when adults are involved. However, parents with very low self-esteem have difficulty with open expression of love feelings even towards their own children. I remember one woman saying to me: 'I'm convinced my children must hate me in the way I hate myself and so I never give them the opportunity of hurting me by telling them that I love them.' In another case a man in his mid-thirties was very concerned to tell his father that he loved him. However, his father had never expressed love to him and he was terrified that his father would laugh at him if he declared his love for him. He had become a mirror of his father. I said to him 'tell me, if your father turned around to you in the morning and said "son, I've been wanting to tell you for years that I love you", how would you feel?' The man's eyes filled with tears and he said 'I'd feel great'. 'So would your father if he heard your declaration', I replied. It took him some time to pluck up the courage but, eventually, he declared his love. The relationship with his father deepened significantly from that moment of intimacy.

Honest, genuine and frequent expression of welfare feelings is paramount for the emotional well-being of the family. There are several stages or steps to the expression of welfare feelings:

- owning the feeling
- sending an 'I' message
- expressing the feeling unconditionally.

○ Own the feeling

If I say to you 'you make me so happy', I am loading you with responsibility for my happiness and I am not recognising that the happy feeling is actually saying something about me, which is that 'I feel happy when I am with you'. Ownership of my feeling also means taking responsibility for it. This implies that if at some stage you decide not to spend some time with me or maybe even choose to leave me, I do not blame you for letting me on my own; I may have difficulty in adjusting to the change but I assure you I am responsible for my own happiness and the last thing I want to do is burden you with the task of making me happy. Regrettably, many people do not own or take responsibility for their own feelings. Partners and children often experience deep guilt arising from feeling responsible for someone who is emotionally dependent. Love lyrics often express such sentiments as:

- 'I can't live without you.'
- 'You're the only one for me.'
- 'You make my dreams come true.'
- 'I'd give up everything for you.'
- 'There is no living without you.'

But these romantic expressions reveal emotional dependence and place an unfair burden on the lover. Rephrasing of romantic sentiment from a stance of ownership and responsibility for one's feelings might lead to the following:

- 'I can live without you.'
- 'I have special feelings for you.'
- 'I feel fulfilled in our relationship.'
- 'I'd give up some things for you.'
- 'There is a lot of living with and without you.'

It is important that children are helped to own and gradually take responsibility for their own welfare feelings. Some parents have said to me: 'My life ended when my child died.' What a burden to put on a small child's shoulder. You are responsible for your own life and you must help your children also to come to that realisation.

○ *Send an 'I' message*

The second step in open expression of welfare feelings is to communicate what you are feeling so that it is clearly a message about you. If you say to me 'did you enjoy the evening?' there is nothing of you in that message and I am left wondering whether you enjoyed the evening. However if you say 'I really enjoyed the evening and hope it was the same for you' at least I know how you felt about the evening and can more safely let you know how I felt about it. Similarly, if you say to a child who has surprised you by cleaning up the kitchen 'you're a great child', there is nothing of what you felt in that message and the child is left wondering whether or not she really impressed you. Were you to speak about yourself and send an 'I' message your response would become: 'I am very pleased and grateful that you cleaned up the kitchen.'

○ *Express feelings unconditionally*

A third aspect to communicating welfare feelings is that there must be no strings attached. If you express love to me and expect the response 'I love you too', you are seeking to manipulate a message of love from me. You have not expressed genuine unconditional feeling for me. If you say 'I really like being with you' but really want me to feel similarly towards you, then again you manifest your dependence and set yourself up for hurt. Suppose I were to reply to your covertly conditional message 'thank you for that but I don't feel the same way'; because of your dependence you are likely to be devastated by the honest reply. Being unconditional is the hardest step of all in expressing welfare feelings.

Because few of us are independent, open expression of welfare feelings can be very threatening to self-esteem. Many of us play it safe or get another to express the feeling for us or wait for the 'right' moment before saying anything or wait for the other to approach us. Very often the feeling does not get expressed at all. The person you are attracted to may also be feeling vulnerable and the opportunity for a relationship gets lost in avoidance behaviours that arise from dependence and lack of confidence. I can certainly recall many such missed opportunities for closeness with others in my own life.

↪ **Expressing emergency feelings**

Emergency feelings act as signals for issues that need expression and resolution. The owning and, when expedient, the revelation of those feelings represent the first steps in a problem-solving process. When, for example, you feel frustrated with a task that is going against you, the frustration may be signifying that:

- You are rushing the task
- You are expecting too much too soon
- You have inadequately planned
- You have not allocated enough time

Acknowledging the presence of the feeling in yourself and owning it as saying something to you about yourself and your needs enable you to make decisions on the actions needed to address the issue involved. Depending on what the underlying problem turns out to be, you may now take one of the following actions:

- Do the task more slowly
- Reduce your expectations
- Return to the planning stage
- Allocate more time to the task

These actions are very different and far more productive than some typical reactions to frustration such as kicking the cat, pounding the table or shouting at yourself or others. When feeling highly frustrated, it is best to leave the task for a period of time, do something relaxing – take a walk, have a cup of coffee, listen to a favourite piece of music – and then, when feeling in charge, return to the task having decided what action is needed.

In the example above, the emergency situation involved only yourself and did not include others. But suppose you are feeling frustrated with the pace of another on a task you have given him to do. The process of discovering the issue underlying the emergency feeling must now include the other. In finding out what your feeling of frustration is telling you, you may need to consider firstly whether:

- You gave clear instructions for executing the task
- You clearly specified a time framework for the task
- You are expecting too much of the other person (expecting him to be as speedy as yourself, for instance)
- You have failed to appreciate that this is a new challenge for the other person

The possibilities are many but in asking yourself the question 'what is the emergency feeling saying to me?' these are the kind of considerations which need to be taken into account. However, suppose you discover that the other person is indeed dilly-dallying and is not making what you consider responsible efforts to complete the task, then you need to express your frustration to him. There are a number of steps in expressing emergency feelings to another:

- Own the feelings
- Send an 'I' message
- Express what is making you feel this way
- Express your need directly and clearly
- Allow the other the freedom to respond or not to respond to your expressed need

Before launching into the expression of an emergency feeling it is wise to first enquire if there is any reason why the desired response is not forthcoming. In the example above, an initial question might be: 'John, I'm wondering if there is something happening that is holding you up in completing the assigned task?' You may find that the person, for example, is worried about some personal or interpersonal crisis, resents being asked to do this task or feels the task is not important enough to merit serious efforts. Whatever emerges, your enquiry has provided the opportunity for the other person to express his emergency feelings and now there is a possibility of resolving the under-lying, hidden issues. Let us suppose that the response to your enquiry is a shrug of the shoulders or a muttered 'there's no problem'. You now need to express your frustration: 'John, I'm feeling frustrated at the minimal effort you are putting into the assigned task and I'm asking that the task be completed by 5.00 p.m. tomorrow.'

All the components of the positive expression of an emergency feeling to another are now present:

- Ownership of the feeling of frustration
- An 'I' message
- Description of what led to the feeling of frustration
- Message which is direct ('John') and clear ('the task be completed by 5.00 p.m. tomorrow')
- Freedom given to the other to respond or not to respond by asking rather than commanding

If you had expressed your frustration aggressively – 'John, what in the name of God is keeping you from completing that task?' – the possibilities of conflict would have been greatly increased. An aggressive message is judgmental and critical, and puts the spotlight totally on the other. By contrast an 'I' message puts the spotlight mainly on yourself.

Many people have difficulties with the last step in the process. Parents often feel they can command children to do things: this creates a very unequal relationship and is a recipe for conflict. But allowing another the freedom to respond or not to respond does not mean allowing that person to slide out of responsibility. There are social responsibilities in every system, be it the family, the classroom, the school, the neighbourhood or the country. Nobody forces me not to drink and drive, not to steal, not to be violent, but if I choose to do any of these socially irresponsible actions then I also choose the sanctions that go with them and so I may lose my driver's licence, be heavily fined or be banned from seeing my family. The process needs to be the same within the family: members must be requested and not forced to carry out reasonable responsibilities, knowing that neglect of these responsibilities may be met with loss of privileges but never the withdrawal of love and regard.

❑ *Responding to feelings*

■ The other person's feelings are not about you

Feelings are the most important route into a family member's inner life; block that access and you may never get to know the other person and you may also block that family member's emotional, social and intellectual development.

It is more likely that you will be able to respond appropriately to any feelings expressed by another when you realise that the other person's feelings are not about you. If you interpret the other person's feelings as being about you then you are likely to react in ways that damage your own and the other's self-esteem. Suppose your wife says to you 'I'm feeling depressed' and you interpret that as 'I'm not good enough for her'. It is easy to see how your reaction may be one of anger, such as 'what do you expect me to do about it?' It is important to understand that her depression is not about you, but about some aspect of herself, perhaps some unmet need or unresolved conflict or insecurity about the future. Only she knows the answer. Do not try to mind-read: for example, 'is it that time of the month?' or 'it probably has to do with your mother's illness'. This way of responding is likely to be experienced as a 'put down' of her feelings. Your partner's depression is an opportunity for her to discover and resolve the crisis that her feeling is signalling. Your role is to stay separate from her feeling in a caring way. Do not take responsibility for your partner but listen to her so she knows you are totally there in a supportive way.

Suppose your partner says 'I'm depressed because I don't feel you love me anymore': is the feeling of depression now about you? The answer is no; she is feeling insecure in the relationship and has a need to know how you feel about her, but it is her need. You now have the choice whether or not to respond to that expressed need.

When anger is expressed the person on the receiving end often hears it as a statement about him. For example, take the situation where an adolescent son returns home late for a meal and the father shouts: 'Where in the hell have you been?' The aggressively expressed anger appears to be about the son who has come home late and, if the boy hears it in that way, he may

storm out, or sit sullenly at the table. However, hearing the anger
as being about him is a misinterpretation of his father's feelings.
If he managed to stay separate, he might have seen that his father's
feeling of anger was about, for example, his need for family
members to be on time for meals or his need for appreciation
to be shown to the person who cooked the meal by being on
time. The anger may be due to deeper hidden issues such as
the father not feeling valued by his son. Who knows? Only the
person who expressed the feeling can say what it is about and
that is his responsibility to discover. From the boy's point of
view, it is important that he acknowledges and apologises for
being late but he must not take on the angry feeling as being
about him. It takes practice to hold on to the fact that other
people's feelings are not about you but are entirely about them.

So far I have been dealing with emergency feelings such as
depression and anger. We may have greater readiness to accept
that another's feelings are not about us when these are emergency rather than welfare feelings. But welfare feelings
are equally entirely about the other. For example, when your
husband says 'you make me so happy' you may want to believe
that this is saying something good about you. But while you
certainly can enjoy the happy feelings of your partner, it is
important to realise that these feelings are a statement about
him not about you. The happiness may be due to having had
more time with you, or having had a particularly intimate
sexual encounter with you or because the garden is looking
wonderful after your hard work. Only he knows the answer.
The issue is that some need of your partner has been met and
he is feeling happy about that. But it is his need and, therefore,
the satisfied feeling is about him. If you believe the feeling is
about you, the danger is that you will take responsibility for
the happiness of the other and will deprive your partner of the
maturation that results from being responsible for his own
feelings and needs. The way to respond here is the same as for
emergency feelings: stay separate, acknowledge that you are
glad the other is feeling happy but do not take on responsibility
for the other person's welfare.

Where children are involved, the last step in responding to
expressed welfare or emergency feelings is different from adults.

As for adults, the feelings are totally about the child expressing them, so the staying separate holds. The second step of acknowledging the child's feelings also holds. However, in the third step the parents rather than the child have to take responsibility for the needs underlying the feelings. As children grow older, this responsibility needs to be gradually handed over to them.

■ Importance of responsiveness to feelings

The way a family responds to the expressed feelings of its members is an important issue for self-esteem development and family harmony. The healthy family is responsive to the expression of all feelings by its members, whereas in unhealthy families feelings may be dismissed, criticised, laughed at, punished or ridiculed. A family member who expresses a feeling may be labelled as, for example, a 'softie', a 'cry baby', 'bold', 'impossible' or 'weak'. All these responses damage the relationships within the family and the self-esteem of each member.

How is emotional responsiveness demonstrated? Take, for example, the child who comes home from school crying. Comforting her with some comment such as 'dear, dear, it will all pass' is not responding to the child's emergency issue. Certainly, you need to comfort the child but, most of all, you need to listen and gently encourage her to talk about what has caused this upset. It may be an overcritical teacher, a bullying experience in school or a fear of your disapproval over some misdemeanour that occurred during the day. It may be something far more serious. What is important is to get to the issue that needs resolution and then help the child to get back into a welfare state. But if you do not listen or you are irritated or dismissive, the child will learn not to approach you with her inner feelings and a serious block to that child's emotional development will be created. On occasions, parents can get annoyed and frustrated with children, but children are very forgiving of these limitations of parents. However, if the negative response to feelings is regular, the child will interpret this as a message about her unworthiness and will learn to hold in feelings rather than risk hurt and rejection. How many of us as children were frightened to tell our parents of unfair, punishing, humiliating and sometimes violent experiences in classrooms and in school yards? Children tend to believe that adults will not help in such situations. Unless parents learn to respond actively and positively to their own emergency feelings, it is unlikely that they will do so when their children express such feelings. If you can see clearly that feelings are merely pointers for change and not statements about worth, you will be able to respond positively to your child's expression of anger, upset, fear or any other feeling.

No matter what the emergency feeling is, it is always a message about change – sometimes minor, sometimes major. If you are feeling lonely and frustrated in a couple relationship then this is a sign that change is needed within that relationship so that you can feel happy and content. If you are unhappy at work then the feeling is letting you know that some aspect of your work life needs to change; maybe you need more challenge, maybe you feel threatened by a colleague, or maybe you want to completely change your career direction. The message of a particular emergency feeling for a person is unique to that person and this applies just as much to children as to adults. Parents, of course, need to help the child to discover what need is not being met. I have met children who are what I call 'face watchers': children who dread that a parent will be moody, cross, irritable, aggressive or violent, or that parents will verbally or physically fight with each other. The child's fear is an indication of her unmet need to feel safe and assured that her needs will be met. It is a terrifying experience for children when they witness frequent open conflict between their parents.

If children's feelings are not responded to in positive ways within the home, they will learn to inhibit the expression of feelings that are punished and, unfortunately, they will carry that timidity or silence into the classroom. The danger then is that failure to express emergency feelings – and indeed, welfare ones – will lead to a host of unmet needs for those children. If the teacher repeats the behaviour of parents by responding negatively to the expression of particular feelings, the child will learn to bottle up her inner experiences all the more. I have encountered a number of children who developed mutism in

the early days of schooling. The mutism was situational, only
occurring with a particular teacher. What typically happened
in these cases was that during the first few days of schooling
the child was homesick, crying for the parents and sometimes
inconsolably tearful. The reaction of the teacher was to shout
at and ridicule the child. Children have very little power and in
these cases their mutiny against being so badly treated was to
retreat into themselves and not risk any further hurt, humiliation or rejection. Children's welfare feelings can also be
inhibited within homes and classrooms. One adult client told
me of his first few days in school when he felt enthusiastic and
eager to please his teacher. He sat in a front desk and eagerly
answered any of the questions the teacher asked until she
reacted at one point by saying 'John, please go to the back of
the class and don't answer any more questions'. This child
never asked another question or showed enthusiasm in a classroom again. Children depend on adults to develop a sense of
themselves; any slight can become so easily magnified in a
developing child's mind.

▪ Positive responding to another's feelings

The positive expression of both welfare and emergency feelings
needs to be responded to in ways that indicate to the sender that:

- he is loved and valued
- there is a genuine desire to hear fully the welfare or emergency message being voiced.

As you have seen, it is important not to collude with inappropriate expressions of feelings. If, for example, your adolescent
son, in response to a request you make of him, says 'go to hell,
I'm not doing that', it is vital that he is not allowed get away
with such an unacceptable response. A sanction is needed here
and a clear statement that such communication is not tolerated
within this family. This must be done when he has calmed down
and when you can deliver the message in a positive but firm
way. Remember, your relationship with your son must remain
intact. What you are correcting is one small bit of behaviour.

Positive responsiveness to expressed feelings involves:

- Giving individual attention to the person expressing the feeling
- Staying separate from the feeling expressed (it is not about you!)
- Trying to discover the need behind the feeling (this may be clear or unclear)
- Using the first name of the sender
- Not taking responsibility for the person or the need (except with children and even here give responsibility when the child is at an age to take it)
- Being supportive and unconditional in your response

An example will clarify this process. If your partner says angrily 'you're never here', it is clear that the emergency feeling of anger is present and that there is some unresolved and unclear issue behind this communication. Listen to and observe carefully both the verbal and non-verbal messages. Most of all do not personalise the message – stay separate. Try to discover the hidden need by warmly and calmly saying: 'In what way am I always out?' Your partner may respond: 'You're never here when I need you.' Stay with the discovery or clarification of the need by responding: 'At what times do you need me?' Now the hidden needs may emerge: for example, 'I hate when you're not home at meal times and I would like you to be there at the children's bed times'. Now the needs have been revealed. You are not responsible for your partner's needs and you have a choice about how you wish to respond. Your response needs to show that your partner has a right to express needs and you value such expression. Your response might be as follows: 'I'm glad you have told me about these needs and I certainly will make greater efforts to be home at the times you're requesting. However, there may be times when I am delayed but I will ring and let you know when this is likely to happen.'

If your partner had expressed an unreasonable need such as 'you should never be late' then a firm response would have been needed. The hidden issue here may be 'I want you to be always on time for me'. The response might then be: 'I'm happy that you like seeing me home on time but there is no way I can guarantee always being on time. There are too many issues that may arise to make that possible. However, I will do my best to contact you when I've been delayed.'

When people express anger something has usually preceded the angry outburst which has hurt, humiliated or threatened them. The angry feeling is 'right' as it provides the person with information and it gives the energy to express the person's right to be respected, valued and accepted as a member of the family. When the anger is expressed aggressively that is not a time for negotiation but a time either to show no response at all or to make a clear statement: 'I want to hear what you are angry about but I will not respond when you shout or roar.' When the person has calmed down, enquire what the anger is all about and help the person to express it in a way that leads to the discovery of the hurt that preceded the anger. The essential point is to respond to all expressions of feelings in a way that lets the other know that you care enough to want to discover which needs are not being met within the family.

Communicating Effectively within the Family

❏ *Communication patterns within unhappy families*

- Judgmental
- Controlling
- Neutral
- Superior
- Certain
- Discrepant
- Double messages
- Too accepting/too critical
- Personalisation
- Scapegoating
- Displacement
- Triangulation
- Myths
- Secrets

❏ *Communication patterns within happy families*

- Active listening
- Non-judgmental
- Permissive
- Empathic
- Equalising
- Provisional
- Direct and clear
- Congruent

It is impossible to overemphasise the immense need humans have to be really listened to, to be taken seriously, to be understood.
Dr Paul Tournier, MD

❏ Communication patterns within unhappy families

The way in which family members communicate with each other reflects and reinforces the pattern of relationships that typically operates between them, whether this be an enmeshed pattern, a neglectful pattern or an unconditional and empathic pattern.

The protective communication patterns described below are typical of enmeshed and neglectful families; the frequency and severity with which they occur depends on the extent, intensity and depth of enmeshment or neglect within the family. The term 'protective' is used deliberately because family members employ these types of communication patterns subconsciously in order to reduce the possibility of hurt and rejection. These ways of communicating are not used to hurt or abuse the other person; they are employed to prevent hurt and abuse happening to oneself. Unfortunately, what one is trying to protect oneself from is unwittingly enacted on the other. For example, if you label me 'stupid' so you can feel superior, you protect yourself by putting the spotlight on me, and you are further protected as I struggle with the humiliation and hurt of the 'put-down' message. Indirectly, however, you have damaged my self-esteem and also maintained your own low self-esteem.

Protective communication patterns	
• Judgmental	• Too accepting/too critical
• Controlling	• Personalisation
• Neutral	• Scapegoating
• Superior	• Displacement
• Certain	• Triangulation
• Discrepant	• Myths
• Double messages	• Secrets

Behind every protective communication there is a hidden message that in troubled families is too risky to declare. While all these kinds of communication serve the purpose of avoiding possible hurt, criticism, humiliation and rejection, unfortunately, because the real message is not voiced, the unhealthy relationship patterns within the family continue. Only when safety is created, through the establishment of supportive, unconditional and caring relationships, will family members be ready to let go of protective communication patterns.

■ Judgmental communication

Judgmental communication is typical of the enmeshed family and is often used by the parent or partner who relates narcissistically to others. Examples of judgmental communication are given below along with the unvoiced message underlying each one.

Judgmental message	Hidden message
• 'You're good for nothing.' • 'You're lazy.' • 'You look awful.'	• 'I want you to love me.' • 'I want you to do certain things for me.' • 'I'm embarrassed when you dress without due care and I would like you to look well.'

You can see from these examples how the hidden messages are more difficult to verbalise than the judgments as they focus on the sender and thus the possibilities of rejection are far higher. The judgmental messages attempt to browbeat the other into submission without the sender having to say anything about herself.

■ Controlling communication

Controlling communication is again typical of the enmeshed family and may be employed by either the person who relates narcissistically or the person who relates overprotectively to others.

Controlling message	Hidden message
Narcissistic relating • 'I'm not asking, I'm telling you to do what I say.' • 'Those colours are all wrong on you.' • 'If I were you this is what I would say.'	 • 'I'm afraid I'm not good enough to request you to do something for me.' • 'I feel excluded by you.' • 'I need you to need me.'
Overprotective relating • 'What's coming over you?' • 'Did you miss your Daddy today?' • 'You never call.'	 • 'I am threatened by the change in you.' • 'I want you to love me.' • 'I feel you are avoiding me.'

You can see that these controlling messages, whether of a narcissistic or overprotective nature, serve to hide the vulnerability of the sender of the message, reduce risk-taking and put the spotlight on the receiver of the message. The self-esteem of the sender is apparently protected while that of the receiver comes under threat.

■ Neutral communication

Neutral communication is frequently used in more extremely enmeshed families and is the most common pattern in very disturbed families, particularly the emotionless family and the symbiotic family. In this type of communication, any show of emotion which threatens the protective relating patterns of the family is 'neutralised' through the receiver of the message showing no emotional response or physically withdrawing or changing the topic of conversation or dismissing the other as being 'overemotional', 'hysterical' or 'selfish'. The show of emotion is threatening to the receiver of the message (usually one or both of the parents or a family member who has identified with the threatened parent) and the safe thing to do is not to respond, or to divert or dismiss. For example, parents who were seriously rejected when they were children are subconsciously convinced of their unlovability and any demonstration of affection from others cannot be trusted in the face of such a sad history. It takes a lot of safety and healing before these people can accept feelings of warmth, affection, love and caring.

■ Superior communication

The person within the family who acts in a superior way is, paradoxically, manifesting an inferiority complex. Superior communication is more common in narcissistic than in other types of relating. The aim is to hide and protect the underlying sense of inferiority from others.

Superior message	Hidden message
• 'I know what is best for you.'	• 'I need you to see me as capable.'
• 'There is nothing I don't know on that subject.'	• 'Please don't see my vulnerability.'
• 'You've come to the right person for help.'	• 'I want you so much to like me.'

As for the other patterns of communication outlined, in these messages the sender's self-esteem is apparently protected, the protective way of relating is reinforced and the other person's self-esteem is undermined.

■ Certain communication

Certain communication is very similar to superior communication. Within the enmeshed family both the parent who relates narcissistically and the one who overprotects can be very definite and rigid in their attitudes: the narcissistic parent can quite categorically assert that it is only right that her needs should come first, while the parent who overprotects can equally firmly say 'your needs are more important than mine'. Symbiotic families also engage in very rigid communication and the basic message that 'we are all the same in this family and it is the family that counts most of all' can be rigorously defended. Similarly, in emotionless families any display of welfare feelings may be ridiculed in no uncertain terms. In all cases, the purpose of certain communication is to support and maintain the protective pattern of relating within the family and, particularly, to protect the very low self-esteem of the parents.

■ Discrepant communication

All protective patterns of communication are distressing but none is more confusing than the discrepant message. Here the person sending the communication is giving one message at a verbal level but another at a non-verbal level. For example, the person who greets you with 'it's good to see you' but maintains a very stern and unwelcoming facial expression is sending a discrepant message. The parent who says to a child 'I love you' but squeezes the child so tightly that it hurts is being discrepant in her communication. Generally speaking, the receiver will note the non-verbal rather than the verbal message. Parents who engage in this type of communication are deeply distressed and create families that are of a most neglectful nature. For these parents the hidden message is 'I don't believe that anyone, even my own child, could really love me'. The discrepant message is designed to disguise the dreadful vulnerability of the sender and to so confuse the receiver that he is left floundering around looking for the real message.

- ### Double messages

The so-called double-bind message has been the subject of much investigation and has been held responsible for the development of schizophrenic behaviours. This type of communication occurs in the most unhappy families. The following example illustrates how it works. The father brings his son a birthday present; the son runs upstairs, opens it and finds two neck ties. Delighted, he puts on one of the ties, rushes downstairs and says 'hey, Dad, look'; his father responds 'you didn't like the other one?' This is the kind of 'no win' situation that can be terribly upsetting to family members. No matter what you do, you cannot please the person who sends you a double message. How does the double-bind message protect? By never allowing the receiver of the message to get emotionally close to the sender. Such closeness would threaten the defensive walls that hide the very frightened child inside the adult who does not want to be hurt anymore. The strategy is very clever – it has to be, as the hurt experienced in the past has been very great.

- ### Too accepting/too critical communication

This communication pattern typically results from the classic combination of an overprotective person married to a narcissistic partner. The overprotective spouse protects herself by always giving in to the other and the narcissistic partner protects himself through a constant barrage of criticism. The passivity is protective because by being always accepting of what the other says, the person prevents further escalation of the hurt being experienced. The person who is excessively critical protects himself through keeping the focus on the other and through leaving the other feeling low and humiliated. He can now maintain the pretence of superiority.

▪ Personalisation

Personalisation is similar to the kind of communication which is too accepting. An example of personalisation is where a family member says 'you're so selfish' and you hear that criticism as being about you rather than as being a message – albeit hidden – about the sender. You may now do one of two things: you may attack back – 'when was the last time you thought about anybody other than yourself?' – or you may withdraw, feeling hurt and angry. It may be easier to recognise how the criticism protects the sender than to see how the personalisation protects the receiver of the message. But by accepting the message as being about you, you protect yourself from further attack and by attacking back you protect yourself even further. Likewise if you withdraw, you cleverly protect yourself from further rejection. Personalising other people's messages is a common phenomenon in all unhappy families.

▪ Scapegoating

Where there is a 'scapegoat' within the family she may act as either the 'punch-bag' or the 'soft touch' for all other family members. The 'punch-bag' is the family member onto whom all other members project their feelings of rejection, frustration, hurt or anger. This person (parent or child) becomes blamed for everything that goes wrong in the family. Once again, this is a clever protective device. When one family member becomes the target of all problems, there is no risk of rejection in the interactions between the other family members. A further protection is that since all the focus is on the scapegoat nobody in the family has to own their own problems. The scapegoat will usually be the family member who is least threatening and whose regard is of least value to the others in the family. This 'punch-bag' type of communication occurs only in grossly disturbed homes. The eldest child in a troubled family frequently becomes the 'punch-bag' for parents' ineptitude.

The second type of scapegoating is where one member of the family becomes the source for the fulfilment of the needs of all the others in the family. Incest is one example of this kind of scapegoating where the 'soft touch' is a child. The 'soft touch' is expected to be always there for others but must never express her own needs. I have worked with women and with men who, both as children and as adults, felt they always had to be there for the rest of the family and dared not say 'no' to any expressed needs or indicate that they had any plans made for themselves. I have met people in their forties and fifties who are unmarried and who are still expected to obey the commands of their ageing parents and other adult family members. Gross neglect has been perpetrated in such families as everybody – most of all, the person who has been scapegoated – has remained stuck with their self-esteem difficulties. Family members who have been scapegoated in this way find it difficult to let go of the role that has been foisted on them as their identity is deeply enmeshed with being 'selfless' and devoted to meeting the needs of others.

■ Displacement

Displacement is similar to scapegoating except that it is not always the same person in the family who is targeted. Of course, displacement does not just occur within families; feelings may be displaced onto people outside the family or onto animals or objects. Displacement may occur with both welfare and emergency feelings. For example, if a spouse's or a child's feelings of love are not reinforced within the family, this person, who now feels hurt and rejected, may displace her feelings of love onto a pet animal or onto somebody outside the family or onto some intense hobby or interest. By displacing the unreinforced welfare feelings onto something or somebody other than the person whose acceptance is important, the person manages to reduce the threat of rejection. Where emergency feelings such as anger, frustration, hurt and resentment are concerned displacement is usually onto persons who pose the least emotional threat or onto animals or objects that cannot lash back. For instance, if a father is aggressively dismissive of a child's need for attention, the child may feel hurt and angry but to express these emergency feelings to the father would mean risking further rejection and so the child may now, for example, punch a younger brother or kick the dog or be vicious during team games.

Displacement may occur in both enmeshed and neglectful families but it is far more common in the latter. When there is gross neglect of the welfare of family members, the danger is very great that the anger such neglect gives rise to will be displaced through violent behaviour onto people outside the family. The more vulnerable members of a community – children who are shy, the elderly, adults who are non-assertive, teachers who are passive – are then at risk.

■ Triangulation

Triangulation is a common protective communication mechanism within distressed families. The protection here occurs through getting unmet needs satisfied by a third party and thereby not confronting the conflict that exists between the two family members involved. An example is where there is emotional distancing between a husband and wife and the husband, in order to satisfy his unmet emotional need to be loved, develops an extramarital relationship with another woman. When the wife discovers the affair, she puts all the blame on the 'other woman'. The 'other woman' becomes the third party and hence the triangle.

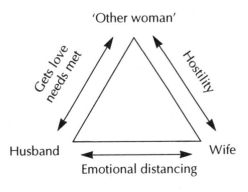

The wife has managed to protect herself from feeling rejected by putting all the blame on the third party. Of course, the real problem is not tackled and the marital conflict remains unresolved.

Sometimes, it is the third party who intervenes in an attempt to divert conflict occurring between two members of a family. A child can often become the third party in a triangle by acting as a 'go-between' in rows between the parents. This situation is typical where there is extreme narcissism or frequent open conflict between parents. Children so depend on their parents that they will do anything to maintain harmony. Through triangulation the child reduces the possibility of parental rows. In very disturbed families, a child may get sick any time he feels conflict is about to erupt between the parents. I have worked with children who suffered asthmatic attacks or pseudo-epileptic episodes when the threat of rows between parents was high. This kind of triangle may be depicted as follows:

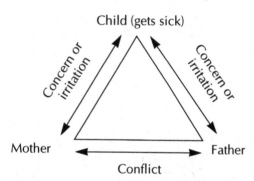

In-laws can often create triangles on issues between a husband and wife or between a parent and a child, thus preventing the real problems from being fully talked through and resolved. One hidden issue here may be that the in-law is afraid of losing control within this family should husband and wife become stronger in their relationship and so the strategy of divide and conquer comes into play. This outside interference must be resisted by the couple involved.

▪ Myths

Another type of protective communication that occurs within unhappy families involves the development of a mythical view of a particular family member. This person is often the one who carries a lot of responsibility within the family and the myth is subconsciously developed in order to reinforce this person's position. A myth within my own family of origin was that 'Tony can always look after himself'. I remember this being said when I was only seven years of age, but the myth strengthened the notion that I was the principal carer within the family and that I did not need any caring myself. This was not true – how could a child of seven look after himself? However, the myth was necessary in order to protect the family from further deterioration.

A very common myth within families is that 'Mother is only happy when the rest of the family is happy'. This myth perpetuates the dependence of all other family members on the mother and maintains her reliance on caring to gain acceptance. The myth then results in a lack of independence and individuality within the family. The myth does, however, protect the mother from rejection and the rest of the family from failure and humiliation.

▪ Secrets

It is amazing the number of skeletons that are lurking in the cupboards of many families. A not uncommon secret within Irish families was where a child's supposed sister was actually the child's mother and the supposed mother was actually the grandmother. The purpose of this secret was to protect the family from feelings of shame. However, the child of such a secret suffers greatly because of the confusing messages within this two-generation family. Children are intuitive and quickly sense that something is wrong. Often, later on, these children subconsciously re-enact the secret by becoming lone parents themselves.

Another secret which can occur within families is keeping the death of a parent hidden from a young child; this secret may often be further complicated by telling the child that the parent has gone to some foreign place and will be returning someday. Later on the revelation of the secret – often by somebody outside the family – can give rise to much upset and consternation. Another quite frequent secret is the cover-up of psychiatric, disability or learning problems of a family member.

Abortion is yet another experience which may become a safely guarded secret within the family or within the woman herself and the woman may suffer for years deep feelings of guilt, shame and fear of discovery. Such suppressed emergency feelings block her from developing closeness with others and, sadly, her own emotional and social life becomes, in turn, aborted.

Incest and sexual abuse can be other closely guarded secrets within the family. The pressure of keeping these experiences secret can lead to extreme behaviours in the child who is being abused. I have worked with children who mutilated themselves or who withdrew into the silent world of mutism or who became destructive of property or sexually promiscuous. These behaviours occur because, unfortunately, when children are physically, emotionally or sexually abused they blame themselves and see themselves as 'bad', 'dirty' or 'unlovable'.

Secrets can also be kept from a particular person in the family by a coalition of other members. A typical example of this is where information is held back from a parent for fear she would get upset or would react aggressively. This cover-up puts considerable strain on those keeping the secret; it also excludes and marginalises the parent from whom the information is being kept.

Ironically, though the aim of secrets is to protect against hurt, rejection, humiliation or aggression, the inevitable outcome is that they cause great hurt within individuals and families.

❏ *Communication patterns within happy families*

Protective patterns of communication are far more common within families than are effective, positive means of communication. This is not surprising when you consider that the kind of communication which occurs in the family reflects the level of self-esteem of individual family members and the nature of the relationships between them. Parents carry their self-esteem problems and unresolved issues from their families of origin into the new family and unless they take the responsibility of changing their feelings about themselves and of separating out from their families of origin, then it is unlikely that positive means of communication will develop within the newly created family. As long as parents themselves fear hurt and rejection they will continue to employ protective communication patterns and their vulnerability will be repeated by their children.

Awareness of constructive means of communication can help parents in their efforts to create a happy family. Such communication will come easy to parents who have high self-esteem, who have a close relationship with each other and who are independent of their families of origin and of others.

Positive communication patterns	
• Active listening • Non-judgmental • Permissive • Empathic	• Equalising • Provisional • Direct and clear • Congruent

■ Active listening

Listening is the first act of communication. Many individuals with whom I have worked worry that, when they are in company, they will run out of things to say. My advice to them is that it is far more important to listen than to talk. When you listen attentively to another, you communicate a number of important messages:

- 'I accept and value you as a person.'
- 'What you are saying deserves my attention.'

In accepting the person you elevate that person's self-esteem and by listening you provide the encouragement for her to continue talking. Furthermore, by putting the emphasis on listening, conversation is far more likely to flow. When you are worried about becoming tongue-tied, you are distracted from the person you are with and you cannot communicate effectively.

Families, typically, do not put enough emphasis on listening. Very often, for example, no sooner has a child got two words out of his mouth than the parent is advising, criticising or talking about herself; communication then breaks down as the child who was talking is likely to feel 'put down' and may withdraw or react aggressively. If you allow the other person as much time as she needs to talk over whatever is pleasing or troubling her, you will begin to discover her inner world of needs, concerns, fears, dreams, wishes and feelings.

In communicating to the other that you are listening attentively two elements need to be considered:

- You need to show that you hear and understand what is being said – this is a cognitive skill.
- You need to show through your body language that your focus is on the person talking – this is a social skill.

You can very effectively communicate that you are listening without ever using words but rather by using body language, for example leaning towards the other, making regular eye contact (not staring), keeping an open body posture (arms unfolded, turned towards the person talking), nodding, smiling or displaying appropriate facial expressions in response to what the other is saying. Non-verbal communication is far more accurate than verbal. You can attempt to fool people with words but the body does not lie. Children are marvellously adept at reading non-verbal communication.

I recall a man in his mid-thirties who told me that as a four-year-old child he stopped asking his mother questions. Young children can plague parents with questions because they are attempting to make sense and order out of a very complex world. This man remembered being in the kitchen asking his mother about this and that. She was busy and kept responding 'yes', 'yes', 'yes', but went on working and made no eye contact with him. He remembered that he said to himself 'she's not listening' and never asked another question. Neither could he go to his father with his questions as he tended to be dour, irritable and aggressive. I actually knew this man's mother and had experienced her as never listening; she talked and talked and talked but rarely gave the other person a chance. Clearly, it was not the one-off experience of 'non-listening' in the kitchen that resulted in the child's withdrawal; his mother rarely listened but it was that morning that he realised this.

In troubled families children learn to watch carefully the faces of the parents in order to create some kind of safety for themselves. Many adults who are insecure also watch the faces of partners or bosses or friends. While children are excellent at reading non-verbal communication, adults tend to focus more on the verbal message and accordingly miss out on the messages underlying the words. As a result, communication can break down much more quickly because the hidden message is what the sender really wants the receiver to hear but is too afraid to express it clearly.

The basis for effective listening is an unconditional acceptance of the person who is talking. Accepting the person in this way does not mean that you agree with everything that is being said but if you do disagree or feel offended or feel put upon, you express this dissatisfaction within the context of a valuing relationship. You do not personalise what the other is saying; rather you focus on the particular issue that is affecting you. For example, if your partner says 'you're late again', you bear in mind that this is not a message about you. Instead you try to get behind the words to the real message coming from your partner which may be something like 'I feel angry when you come in late and I need you to stick to the time commitment made to me'. If you had personalised the message, you might have reacted by saying something like 'you always have something to complain about' and such a reaction means listening has ceased, misinterpretation has occurred and communication has been blocked.

Effective listening is ensured by practising the following:

- Unconditional acceptance of the person talking
- Attending fully to what the person is saying in order to understand what she is attempting to communicate
- Sending non-verbal messages that communicate you are really interested in the person and in what she is saying
- Asking for clarification when you are unsure of what is being said

- Owning and relaying your reactions to what is being said in a way that maintains the valuing relationship
- Being patient and giving time to the other to talk out what is pleasing or troubling her

If you are unsure of what the other person is trying to say, it is important to the listening process that you seek to clarify what is really being said. Such enquiries are further evidence of your efforts to listen and reassure the person communicating with you. Examples are:

- 'Could you repeat what you've just said to me.'
- 'I'm not totally clear about what you are saying and wonder could you elaborate on it for me.'
- 'Let me just check with you, what you need is . . .'

■ Non-judgmental communication

In non-judgmental communication, when a family member's behaviour is being commented upon – either positively or critic-ally – it is the behaviour that is the target and not the person. Furthermore, the person communicating owns what she is saying as being about herself and not about the other.

When you engage in non-judgmental communication you:

- Avoid labelling (for example 'You're insensitive', 'You're bad', 'You're selfish', 'You're so good', 'You're aggressive')
- Avoid blaming (for example 'You're always late', 'You're always at your brother', 'You're just thinking about yourself', 'You're getting above yourself, young lady')
- Own what you want to say to the other as being about you

Examples are:

- 'I'm not happy with your homework and I need you to write it out more legibly' (in response to poorly done homework)
- 'I am so pleased with how well you have cleaned the kitchen' (in response to child cleaning kitchen)
- 'I'm concerned that I have so little time with you' (in response to partner being late again)

- 'I feel angry when I see you hitting your brother and I'm asking you not to do that again' (in response to older child hitting younger child)
- 'I would be worried and anxious if you were to get a motor bike' (in response to seventeen-year-old child wanting a motor bike)
- 'I feel you are not old enough to go to an unsupervised late-night disco' (in response to fifteen-year-old child demanding to go to late-night disco)

Non-judgmental communication ensures that the self-esteem of both persons is enhanced; the message being communicated is clear; the relationship between the two persons remains intact; and communication remains open to further negotiation.

■ Permissive communication

Permissive communication is the direct opposite of controlling communication where the person communicating attempts to dominate and take power over the other. Permissive communication allows others to express their own views, opinions, beliefs and feelings and to do things in their own way.

When you engage in permissive communication you:

- Avoid dominating and controlling the other
- Avoid giving advice unless it is requested
- Avoid criticising the other's behaviour
- Avoid manipulating the other to get your own way
- Give permission to yourself to express whatever needs to be communicated
- Give permission to the other to be expressive of views, needs, feelings etc.
- Do not personalise the other's message but recognise it as being about that person

Examples are:

- 'Mary, I am interested to hear your point of view on what school Johnny should go to next year.'

- 'I'm really glad that you've told me how unhappy you've been about my being away so often.'
- 'I really would prefer if you would make up your own mind on how you would like this job done.'
- 'What is your opinion on this issue?'
- 'My view on this matter is . . . what do you think?'

Permissive communication provides each member of the family with the freedom and the safety to express whatever needs to be revealed. This permissiveness shows belief in one's own capability and in the capability of the other and thus adds considerably to the self-esteem of both. It provides for openness in relationships and is the launch-pad for the satisfaction of needs and the resolution of individual and family problems.

■ Empathic communication

An empathic response to the other person's message is essential to effective communication. If you respond coldly or without feeling, communication quickly breaks down. Once others see that you are empathic in your response they will continue to talk. Empathic communication creates the needed safety for the revelation of all feelings, both welfare and emergency: it is safe to say 'I love you' and it is safe to say 'I feel angry'.

When you engage in empathic communication you:

- Express clearly any feelings that need to accompany your message to others
- Allow others to express any feelings that need to accompany their messages to you
- Show a positive emotional response to the display of welfare or emergency feelings from others
- Hear the message from others as saying something about them not about you

Examples are:

- 'I'm really sorry you are upset by what has happened.'
- 'I'm thrilled that you've told me you love me.'

- 'I can understand that you feel angry about my being late.'
- 'Tell me more about how worried you are.'
- 'It's okay to feel sad and disappointed about not getting higher marks in your exam.'
- 'I really want to hear what is upsetting you.'

It can be seen that empathic responding elevates your own and the other person's self-esteem, creates stronger bonds between you and ensures that the doors of communication remain open.

■ Equalising communication

When you engage in equalising communication you:

- Value and respect your own messages
- Value and respect the messages of others
- Avoid being superior
- Affirm and encourage others to express themselves

Examples are:

- 'I'm sure you can come to a decision on that yourself.'
- 'I've given my point of view but I would value hearing your views.'
- 'We can sort out this matter together.'

The clear message here is that the other is capable and deserving of respect and that what she says is as worthy of being listened to as what anyone else has to say. In this case the boost to self-esteem is enormous, the relationship is equalised and communication is made easier.

■ Provisional communication

Unlike the 'I'm always right' type of communication, provisional communication allows for the possibility of right or wrong on both sides. The person who communicates provisionally does not seek to impose her own views and certainties on another.

When you engage in provisional communication you:

- Assert your own views and opinions
- Respect the views and opinions of others
- Are provisional in asserting views

Examples are:

- 'This is what I believe, but I'm open to being corrected.'
- 'I'm sure there are other ways this matter could be approached.'
- 'Feelings are neither right nor wrong but mere expressions of what is happening to you or me right now.'
- 'This is the way I learned to do this but I'm happy to be shown another way.'

Provisional communication creates an environment where all family members are allowed to have their own opinions, beliefs and ways of doing things and where, if differences arise, there is explanation and negotiation on the matter. The decision may be to agree to differ, or a compromise may be reached or one person may come to realise that she was too tunnelled in her vision on the issue. All the time the relationship remains positive and the issue is discussed calmly and respectfully.

■ Direct and clear communication

In many ways direct and clear communication embraces all the preceding positive communication patterns. With this type of communication there is no confusion about who the message is about, who the message is being sent to, or what the message is saying.

When you engage in direct and clear communication you:

- Own the message as being about yourself
- Direct it clearly to a particular person
- Are clear in what is being communicated
- Use an 'I' message

Examples are:

- 'John, I worry when you do not let me know where you are and I need to be able to contact you when necessary.'
- 'Michael, I feel angry when you put me down in front of others and I'm asking that you do not do it again.'
- 'Mary, I'm really happy to see you again.'
- 'Jane, I would like you to tidy your room please.'
- 'Mark, I miss you when you are away.'
- 'Margaret, I'm not willing to cook a meal until you have tidied up the kitchen after you.'

What happens if you have communicated clearly and directly but no response is forthcoming to your reasonable and fair request? Suppose, for example, that Margaret has not tidied the kitchen in spite of your request. Actions always speak louder than words. But, before resorting to action, it is wise to enquire why your request has not been met. If all you get in response to your enquiry is a shrug of the shoulders, then you need to follow through by not cooking the meal. This action shows that you are serious about your expressed need and indicates your determination not to collude with the other's irresponsible behaviour.

You need to be very sure of yourself to communicate directly and clearly. Nevertheless, all families need to aspire to this kind of communication because it ensures expression of and response to needs and feelings, the elevation of self-esteem and the deepening of emotional bonds.

■ Congruent communication

In congruent communication there is consistency between what you are saying verbally and what you are expressing nonverbally. It is disconcerting and confusing when there is a contradiction between the verbal and non-verbal messages. When communication is congruent the receiver feels safe in responding to the message being sent. Examples are:

Verbal	Non-verbal
• 'I'm happy to be here with you.'	• Smiling, relaxed and open posture
• 'I'm feeling angry right now.'	• Cross facial expression, tightened body, firm eye contact
• 'I am really worried about my exams.'	• Worried facial expression, strained tone of voice, uptight posture

Awareness and practice of positive patterns of communication is the responsibility of each family member but, most of all, of each parent. The model given by the parents sets the scene for the rest of the family.

CHAPTER 9

Developing Responsibility within the Family

❑ *Who does what in the family*
❑ *Behavioural control: a responsibility for all family members*
  ▪ Undercontrol behaviours
  ▪ Overcontrol behaviours
  ▪ In-control behaviours
  ▪ Self-control and the positive use of sanctions
❑ *Unconditional loving and responsibility*

It was like a revelation to me, taking complete responsibility for one's own actions.
Cary Grant

❑ *Who does what in the family*

Who does what within a family can be a major influence on the welfare of that family. There are certain essential family tasks which if neglected lead to all sorts of problems. These necessary tasks have to be repeatedly addressed if a family is to function effectively:

- The provision of material resources (for example, food, clothing, housing, heat and money)
- The provision of affection, comfort, reassurance and support for members of the family
- Sexual gratification of adult partners
- The provision of opportunities for the development of life skills (for example, education of children, career development of both parents, resources for interests and hobbies of each family member)
- Maintenance and management of the family system. This entails management tasks such as leadership (not dictatorship!) and

decision-making and tasks associated with maintaining family
boundaries (not allowing others to interfere with the family)
and with the development of fair and reasonable standards
of behaviour

Traditionally, particular roles were assigned to the mother
and father of the family. The provision of resources and the
maintenance of the family system were the domain of the male
parent while the provision of nurturance and support and the
creation of opportunities for the development of life skills were
seen as the realm of the female parent. The satisfaction of
sexual needs tended to be more a joint affair, but frequently men
saw women as there to satisfy their needs and did not consider
that their wives too had sexual needs. Such stereotyping has
caused and still causes many problems within families. Being
with children all day can be much more difficult than working
outside the home, but some men do not see it as their role to
feed, nurture and comfort children and so women may be over-
burdened by these tasks and feel let down by their spouses.

Nowadays, there is a slow but definite shift towards a more
equal sharing of family responsibilities. In addition, there is
greater recognition that material resources are there for the self-
development of each family member and not just for the male
children or the father. The equal rights of female children and
of mothers to their own social, emotional, career and personal
development are gradually being integrated into family systems.

While it is mothers who are typically overburdened with
family functions, it sometimes happens that children are unduly
laden. It is unreasonable to expect a child to take a leadership
role in the family or take over the caring of younger siblings:
these responsibilities are more appropriate for the parents or
adult carers of children. Unfortunately, however, it is not an
uncommon experience for the eldest girl or boy to be loaded with
such responsibilities. Certainly, from an early age children should
be given specific responsibilities within the family (such as
clearing away their toys, washing and dressing themselves, light
household chores) but they must not be given an adult role.

Many women, as children, experienced being burdened with
domestic responsibilities and then, as adults, continued their

'caring role', rarely seeing their own rights and needs. These are the 'women who love too much', the women whose identities are tied up with caring for others and whose neglect of self can be very great. Often their daughters repeat the 'martyr' role and their sons repeat the 'spoilt' role. It is important that essential tasks within families are appropriately spread out among family members. The healthy family adequately fulfils these tasks and has fair allocation of responsibilities. Families are at risk when these necessary functions are not being adequately met or when one member of the family is overburdened.

❑ *Behavioural control: a responsibility for all family members*

The term behavioural control refers to how the members of a family carry out their respective responsibilities. These responsibilities have been considered in detail throughout this book and can be briefly summarised as follows:

- Development of unconditional, loving interactions
- Resolution of family problems in ways that restore family harmony
- Positive responsiveness to the expression of all feelings
- Clear and direct communication
- Meeting each other's reasonable needs
- Development of acceptable social behaviour

Parents, once again, need to take the lead here and must demonstrate control over all aspects of their behaviour. Children imitate their parents, particularly their actions, and parents' words often fall on deaf ears when they do not match the parents' actions. The parent who frequently loses control with a partner or child is hardly in a position to expect other family members to control themselves. Very often, double standards operate within families wherein a dominating, irritable and aggressive parent expects everybody else to be responsible. Parents who are passive and tight-lipped in the face of irresponsible behaviours on the part of themselves or other members of the family also fail to model responsible control for children.

■ Undercontrol behaviours

It is important for family members to realise that when someone is out of control and responds critically and aggressively to another, that person is, in fact, giving control away. If there is such a person in the family, the other members begin to learn that they can 'get at' this person. Sometimes, a family member's behaviour may be extremely trying (and the person involved is not always a child!) and the responsibility to stay in control may be severely tested. When such a situation arises it is always best to remove yourself from the person who is out of control. The last thing you want to do is add fuel to fire by becoming out of control yourself. An aggressive response will breed either more hostile behaviour on the part of the offender or, possibly, hostile withdrawal. Aggression on your part will certainly undermine family relationships.

When a member of the family is frequently finding it difficult to control any aspect of his behaviour, his irresponsible responses are clear indicators that there are problems – either within the individual concerned or between family members or both – that need resolution. Professional help may be needed. The important issue is not to let undercontrol behaviour on the part of any family member persist for long before seeking help. The persistent manifestation of undercontrol behaviours must not go unconfronted.

Checklist of undercontrol behaviours within families

- Throwing temper tantrums
- Shouting
- Ordering, dominating, controlling
- Using sarcasm and cynicism
- Ridiculing, scolding, criticising
- Labelling each other (for example, 'bonehead', 'stupid', 'lazy', 'ugly', 'animal', 'goodie-good')
- Threatening to leave home, hurt oneself, hurt another, kill oneself
- Threatening (by parents) to send children away ➤

- Parents physically threatening children
- Being physically violent (parent to child, child to child, child to parent, parent to parent, family members to outsiders)
- Being impatient and intolerant with regard to differences between each other
- Assigning punishment out of proportion to misdemeanour involved
- Pushing, pulling, shoving
- Comparing one family member with another or with an outsider
- Having an obvious favourite in the family
- Not calling each other by first names
- Using hostile nicknames
- Being too strict
- Expecting too much of each other
- Showing little or no interest in each other's welfare
- Overeating
- Overdrinking
- Worrying and fretting
- Overspending
- Destroying, selling or stealing family possessions
- Driving car or motor bike or bicycle dangerously
- Letting family members slide out of responsibility
- Not demonstrating affection to each other
- Punishing mistakes and failures
- Never apologising for mistakes
- Not saying 'please' or 'thank you' to each other
- Parents being inconsistent and unpredictable in their responses to their own and their children's irresponsible behaviours
- Allowing one family member (parent or child) to control or hold the family to ransom
- Using withdrawal of love as a weapon to control another family member
- Using hostile silences and sulking to control another family member

■ Overcontrol behaviours

Overcontrol behaviours within a family mean that neglect of family members is ignored, passively accepted, colluded with or kept secret. I have come across families where one of the parents or a relative was aware of gross abuse of a family member but nothing was done to protect the victim. The reason for turning a blind eye lay in the poor self-esteem of the adults concerned. So many times I have encountered the family anthem 'for peace sake don't upset your father' even though he is the one who is physically and emotionally abusive, overdrinking, spending money that is needed for more essential needs, missing work and neglecting the marital relationship. No matter what the reason for overcontrol behaviours, the result is always some neglect of family members. Fortunately, there are now many more support services available to adults and children alike when either they themselves or others are being victimised.

Checklist of overcontrol behaviours within families

- Being timid and fearful
- Passively accepting abusive responses towards oneself or other family members
- Turning a blind eye to neglectful behaviours
- Always trying to please other family members
- Keeping physical or emotional or sexual abuse secret
- Possessing rigid and inflexible attitudes that result in neglect of others (for example 'your father must always be served first')
- Always putting the needs of others before one's own
- Never saying 'no'
- Withdrawing into silences following conflict or failure to have needs met
- Sulking
- Passively colluding with abuse of one family member by another
- Being 'tight-lipped' when emergency feelings (for example, anger, sadness, resentment, fear) need expression
- Resorting to drug-taking (prescribed or otherwise) as a 'way out' of feeling bad
- Elective mutism
- Not expressing needs

■ In-control behaviours

Throughout this book you have seen the devastating effects that the persistence of undercontrol and overcontrol behaviours can have on families. The ability to be in control of yourself is an essential parenting skill. The follow-on skill is to help children to take control of their own behaviour. A surprising revelation for many parents is that it is not their job to control children. It is an invitation to conflict to have one family member control another. As an adult, you know that you would resent being controlled by another; should anyone try to control you, you would feel hurt, helpless, angry and resentful and you might even want to lash back at the source of the control. The same holds for children.

Effective behavioural control within a family is based on the principle that each family member is responsible for his own self-control. Therefore, it is not the task of parents to control children but it is their responsibility to educate children to take responsibility for themselves. Parents have the extra responsibility of ensuring that children do not slide out of learning self-control. The self-control or in-control behaviours that all family members need to practise are outlined below.

Checklist of in-control behaviours within families
• Remaining patient, calm and relaxed in the face of difficult behaviours • Listening to all sides • Being tolerant of differences between family members • Requesting rather than ordering • Saying 'please' and 'thank you' • Addressing each other by first names • Asking permission when wanting to use or borrow another's property • Taking care of each other's property • Showing concern for each other • Responding positively to mistakes and failures • Praising and encouraging effort not performance →

- Regularly affirming the goodness and worth of each other
- Not living life through each other
- Being fair, just, consistent and predictable in punishing misdemeanours
- Having realistic expectations of each other
- Valuing the uniqueness of each family member
- Being flexible in applying family rules for interpersonal conduct and domestic and other responsibilities
- Showing interest in each other's welfare
- Creating safety for the expression of feelings and problems
- Apologising when wrong
- Maintaining close relationships with each other while resolving conflicts
- Being fair in allocating family responsibilities
- Having a healthy diet
- Using financial resources fairly
- Driving all vehicles carefully
- Knowing when help and support are needed

▪ Self-control and the positive use of sanctions

As outlined above, each family member has certain responsibilities to ensure that caring, safety, fairness, justice, order and harmony are created within the family. Failure to meet these responsibilities by any family member must be met not with undercontrol or overcontrol responses, but by the positive use of sanctions. Double standards can often operate within families when it comes to the use of sanctions, where parents feel that it is quite in order to employ sanctions when children are irresponsible but rarely apply sanctions to their own irresponsible behaviours. This is unjust. When children see parents applying sanctions to themselves, they are much more likely to accept sanctions.

The purpose of sanctions is to ensure that family members adhere to agreed responsibilities. The sanction, preferably, is a pre-determined consequence to a specific irresponsible action.

The family member who engages in the unacceptable behaviour then knows that he is choosing to risk being sanctioned. Family members may try to blame one another for the imposed sanction but it needs to be firmly pointed out that no sanction would have occurred if a reasonable choice had been taken. Children learn quickly that reasonable behaviour gains them privileges and that unreasonable actions lose them privileges. Children also begin to realise that it is they who choose the risk of sanction when they act in an irresponsible way.

A sanction must never involve the withdrawal of love, respect and belief in the other: the relationship must always remain the first priority. Nevertheless, the unacceptable action must not go unconfronted. The implementation of a sanction must be done in such a way that the family member knows precisely:

- how he has been irresponsible, and
- what exactly is required of him.

Sanctions are employed to educate for responsibility; they are not a means of controlling or 'putting down' the other person. The positive use of sanctions has certain clear characteristics:

1. When possible, *the sanction applied should be the natural result of the irresponsible action*. Where parents are concerned, the most potent natural sanction is the realisation that their neglectful behaviour will put a strain on each other and their children and may damage the self-esteem of the victim of the neglect. The more parents become aware of their immense power to do 'good' or 'ill' for their children and each other, the less likely they will be to perpetuate neglect. Where children are concerned, some examples of natural sanctions include getting them to tidy up if they have messed up a room, or taking food away from them if they begin to mess with it.

2. *Sanctions need to be specific.* It is pointless, for example, to say to a child 'if I catch you playing ball on the street, I'll kill you', or to say to your partner 'I'll never talk to you again, if you don't remember my birthday'. These threats will be

ignored because neither child nor partner believes that you will carry out such extreme sanctions. Be clear and specific: 'if I catch you playing ball on the street, I'll take your football away for a week', 'if you forget my birthday, I'll feel hurt and I will take myself out for the night to celebrate it'.

3. *Sanctions need to be predictable and consistent.* This means that family members always know where responsibility lies and know that breaching that line will inevitably lead to the application of a sanction. Furthermore, family members need to know that no matter who is involved the same sanction will apply. For example, being on time for meals is an important responsibility in a family. Family members need to know that if they are late for meals without a reasonable excuse the rest of the family will eat without them and the meal will not be kept warm for them.

4. *Sanctions need to be fair.* The sanction must fit the irresponsibility. When sanctions are agreed by the whole family and not left to the whim of one member, the possibility of injustice is considerably lessened. The family should regularly review the responsibility system to guard against unfairness.

5. *Sanctions need to be impersonal.* The family member who loses his temper with another for being irresponsible and then assigns a sanction that arises from frustration will not be effective in communicating his dissatisfaction. The person at the receiving end will know that the sanction is only an outlet for the other person's dependence and frustration, and will blame the other rather than self.

6. *Sanctions need to emphasise what is expected of family members* so that they become opportunities for developing more reasonable behaviour and self-control. Some examples of expectations are given below.

Expectations that family members may have of each other

- Being on time for meals
- Rising from bed when called (only call once)
- Being hygienic
- Eating food slowly and without noise   →

- Asking to be excused when rising from dining table
- Walking in an orderly way around the house
- Doing homework at designated times
- Communicating in respectful ways
- Respecting and taking care of other people's property
- Not using other family members' belongings without permission
- Speaking at an acceptable volume
- Having music or TV at an acceptable volume
- Responding positively to reasonable requests
- When distressed or angry requesting personal time
- Playing in a way that is safe
- Keeping common rooms and own personal space tidy and clean
- Accepting fairly allocated domestic responsibilities (for example, setting dining table, washing up after meals, bringing in fuel, putting soiled clothes in laundry basket)
- Negotiating differences in a calm and valuing way
- Remembering special occasions (for example, birthdays, anniversaries)

7. *Sanctions are best withheld until it is clear why the family member engaged in the irresponsible behaviour.* Sometimes, when the cause of a misdemeanour is discovered, comforting rather than sanctioning may be needed. For example, if your son should respond to a request by saying 'go to hell, I'm not doing that' and this is not characteristic of him, it would be wise to withhold the sanction. Later, when he is calm, talk to him and enquire what led to the hurtful response; you might learn, for example, that he had been badly treated by a teacher in front of his peers and came home feeling angry and humiliated, and that these unresolved feelings triggered his response.

8. *Sanctions need to be positively and calmly applied* so that the family member concerned does not become fearful of the person applying the sanction. A child, or adult, who is frightened may agree to anything but, when he recovers,

nothing will have been resolved and the next irresponsible action may be worse than the first.

9. *Address family members by their first names when applying sanctions.*

What sanctions are available within the family? A list of possibilities is given below but different families demand different solutions and each family needs to determine the most effective responsibility system for its unique circumstances.

Possible sanctions for families

- Positive and firm request for reasonable behaviour
- Deprivation of privileges (the possible loss of a favourite activity can become a strong motivator for responsibility). This can be either self-applied or applied by another
- Withdrawal of attention from the irresponsible action (this is frequently effective, as the ploy can be to get attention)
- Detention with a meaningful purpose. Again this can be self-applied. With children such detention needs to be supervised and the supervisor needs clear and specific directions on what task has been assigned to the child (for example, tidy up a room, complete the wash-up, complete homework)
- Assignment of domestic responsibility (for example, cook meal, cut grass, clean windows, take out fire ashes)
- Warning of deprivation of some future privilege (for example, night out with friends, going to football match, staying overnight with friends, going to cinema to see new popular release)
- Deprivation of pocket money (for children) or donating spare money to charity (for adults)

❏ *Unconditional loving and responsibility*

When family members unconditionally value each other they will not allow each other to slide out of responsibility. Love and responsibility go hand in hand. Unconditional loving not only means acceptance, care, affirmation and the absence of comparisons but also encouragement of responsibilities that build self-esteem. For example, if you observe your adolescent son kicking your younger son and there is a clear expectation in your home that family members treat each other positively and that violence is a non-negotiable issue, you need to correct your son's unacceptable behaviour, but in a way that does not damage his self-esteem or your relationship with him. An altogether too typical reaction is to hit the adolescent or shout aggressively 'pick on somebody your own size', or push him out of the room. All of these responses will damage your son's self-esteem and the relationship between you. They are aggressive and are repeating exactly what you are attempting to correct. This, of course, will be seen by your son as illogical and hypocritical and he is unlikely to learn anything from your responses. If you want your son to be responsible and to increase his level of self-esteem, ask him firstly what led to his violent outburst. He may say that his younger brother was needling him (which is not unlikely). You can now show understanding that such needling can be annoying but ask him whether he feels his brother's behaviour justified a kick. Ask him what he could have done that would have been effective in dealing with his brother's annoying behaviour. He may list possible responses such as ignore him, go to another room, give a warning to stop or withdraw a promised privilege. Let him know now that you believe that he can learn to act more appropriately in the future as a result of the unpleasant experience. At this stage you can apply a sanction, reminding him that its purpose is to ensure responsibility in his relationships with his brother and other family members. This may appear to be an elaborate way to correct your son's behaviour but the benefits are great:

- your son's self-esteem remains intact
- your relationship with him is enhanced
- you have helped him to see where his responsibilities lie.

Unfortunately, parents tend not to talk to children, but instead to direct, command, advise, scold, correct, judge and label them. Neither do parents invite children to give their point of view. If they did so they would find that children know when they have been attempting to slide out of responsible behaviour. Parents need to let their children know that they cannot countenance such behaviour because it would be an act of neglect on their part.

Generally, when you want to encourage responsible behaviours in family members, it is important to avoid messages such as 'you're a wonderful man', 'you're a great partner', 'you're a good girl' or 'you're a clever boy'. The implication of these messages is that the wonder, greatness, goodness or cleverness of the person is tied up with a particular responsible action and is dependent upon its presence. It is more accurate to praise the particular action that has impressed you. For example, instead of saying 'you're a wonderful man', it is more valuable for your partner's self-esteem to say 'John, I am so pleased you remembered my birthday'. Equally it is important to correct only the irresponsible action that has distressed you. To say 'you're a bold boy', 'you're so selfish' or 'you're so aggressive' damages the self-esteem of the person addressed. So, for example, instead of saying 'you're a bold boy', it is more constructive to say 'Michael, I want you to tidy up all of the toys you have scattered around the sitting room'.

Fostering Individuality within the Family

> *To have one's individuality completely ignored is like being pushed quite out of life. Like being blown out as one blows out a light.*
> Evelyn Scott

❏ *Individuality and self-esteem*

Your sense of self-esteem forms the core of your individuality and independence as a person. When family members have self-esteem problems, their sense of uniqueness and individuality is blurred and unless self-esteem change occurs this confused sense of identity will perpetuate. A positive outcome of the happy family is that each member has a strong sense of individuality and high self-esteem. These characteristics are the *sine qua non* for you to effectively leave the family and establish your own independent life.

■ Self-image and the ideal self

Self-image is the end product of family relationships. Whether or not the family is aware of it, every interaction gives some message about a family member's value. These interactions communicate messages about how individual members are viewed along the dimensions of:

- lovable/unlovable
- capable/incapable.

A simple interaction such as an aggressive demand to 'pass the salt' says something about how the sender of the message views herself and, indirectly, the receiver of the message. Because few people have high self-esteem, most will interpret an aggressive message as a 'put down', a manifestation of dislike or an indication of being valueless in the sender's eyes. The self-image of both the sender and the receiver is now adversely affected by the aggressive message. Conversely, a polite request to 'please pass the salt' elevates the self-image of both the sender and the receiver. Self-image is developed through the looking glass of how others perceive you and your interpretation of received messages as positive or negative.

Children believe that parents are always right. They see them as gods and goddesses and they depend totally on them for their view of themselves. When children experience critical, blaming, ridiculing, scolding and 'put-down' messages, they will begin to form an image of themselves as 'a nuisance', 'stupid', 'inadequate', 'falling short', 'never good enough', 'lazy', 'ugly', 'unlovable' and so on. Through a similar process, when parents make demands, set high expectations, impose certain standards of behaviour (for example, cleanliness, tidiness) and want certain personal characteristics exhibited (for example, good looks, intelligence, athleticism), this forms the looking glass through which children form an ideal of how they ought to be if they want to gain love, recognition and acceptance from their parents. If there is a wide gap between children's self-image and their ideal self, then self-esteem difficulties emerge. It is easy to see how traumatising and threatening it is for a child when, on the one hand, parents are saying 'you're not good enough' and, on the other hand, are demanding that 'you should be perfect'. Other examples are given below of where a gap exists between the image the child is given of himself and the ideal standard being held up:

- 'You're stupid: be clever.'
- 'You're ugly: be handsome.'
- 'You're messy: be clean and tidy.'
- 'You're selfish: look after me.'
- 'You're weak: stand up for yourself.'
- 'You're awkward: be skilful.'
- 'You're so slow: be quick.'
- 'You're too quiet: talk up.'

In some families, because of either neglect or overprotectiveness, no ideals are set for children, resulting in lack of motivation and ambition and a sense of apathy and helplessness. Realistic ideals are essential for children to feel challenged. Without challenge children are unlikely to experience a fulfilling life.

While children are totally the victims of the messages they receive from adults, adults themselves have the potential to stay separate from the messages of others and to see these messages as indicators of the self-esteem of the sender. However, you need to have high self-esteem to maintain such objectivity, and hypersensitivity to criticism is, in fact, a much more common phenomenon among adults. This sensitivity to the messages of others reveals dependence and self-esteem difficulties. In effect, most adults are still like children in that they depend on others for their view of themselves. Consequently, for these adults, as for children, the responses of others determine their self-image and the ideals they set for themselves. Examples of contradictory messages that can create a strain between self-image and ideal self within partners in a couple relationship are:

- 'You're never here: be here always for me.'
- 'You're stupid: it's your job to look after our finances.'
- 'You're always complaining: speak up for yourself.'

- 'You're no good at making decisions: take responsibility.'
- 'You hate sex, don't you?: be a good lover.'
- 'You think you know everything: you have to make the decisions.'
- 'You're untrustworthy: be totally honest with me.'
- 'You're impossible to live with: don't ever leave me.'
- 'You're selfish: meet my needs.'

❏ *The effects of self-esteem difficulties on individuals*

As mentioned, self-esteem difficulties arise within family members when there is a wide discrepancy between how they see themselves (self-image) and what others expect of them (ideal self). These difficulties can have marked effects on the well-being of the children, parents and the family as a whole. The level of self-esteem of the parents is the major determinant of the self-esteem development of each other and of children.

▪ Effects on children

When children are faced with a threatening gap between how they see themselves and what others and they themselves expect, then a variety of protective behaviours are developed to reduce the possibility of further hurt and rejection. Typically, children resort to one of the following protective reactions:

- avoidance
- compensation
- rebelliousness
- apathy.

↝ Avoidance

Many children from troubled families find refuge from hurt and rejection by avoidance of any behavioural efforts that might fail to meet a parent's expectations. The child who is always out of the house has developed a wise strategy to protect against parents' rejecting reactions; with little or no presence in the home, there can be little or no failure. Some children become shy and withdrawn so that no demands are made of them; again the wisdom of the strategy is that with no demands there can be no failure, and no failure means no rejection. Other children become totally absorbed in some interest or hobby as a means of avoiding demands that put them emotionally at risk. Yet other children resort to making only minimal efforts and never venturing above average performance as failure is more risky within the higher range. Many parents are puzzled by children who use avoidance strategies; they see that the child has the potential to learn but find that neither ridicule, punishment nor praise succeeds in moving the child out of his protective shell. But, for a child, it is the lesser of two evils to risk disapproval due to lack of effort than to risk rejection due to failure to measure up to the ideals set for him.

I recall a seventeen-year-old girl who was sent to me because she wanted to drop out of school. When I asked her why, she said 'because I won't get all As in my Leaving Certificate examination'. The dilemma for the girl was the gap between her self-image and ideal self:

- 'You're not very clever: be perfect and get high results.'
  (*self-image*)   (*ideal image*)

Later on in the session, when I suggested she read a particular book, she replied 'I've never completely read a book'. The reason she gave for this was that when she could not remember clearly what she had read the day before, this convinced her she was 'not very clever' and put the ideal of 'being perfect' way beyond her. Consequently, she learned to avoid reading books and this strategy had begun in the early years of her school life. Interestingly, she spent hours practising the piano as this was the one area where she managed to meet the 'ideal' expectations of her parents. With the excessive piano practice she was employing a second protective strategy known as compensation.

Another young person I encountered was sent to me because he was stealing considerable sums of money. His father had left home when he was three years of age and had maintained no contact since then. His mother had a strong work ethic, was uncomfortable with intimacy and spent most of her time at work. Her contradictory messages to her son were: 'you never please me' and 'be strong'. He told me that he spent most of his childhood outside the home and had attempted to gain recognition and approval through his peer group. The stealing was subconsciously motivated by a need to please his peer group and the money was used in attempts at 'buying' their approval.

Children also learn to avoid expressing certain feelings if they have been given the contradictory messages of:

- 'You're weak if you show fear or sadness: be strong.'

       (*self-image*)   (*ideal image*)

⤳ Compensation

A clever means by which children seek to resolve the gap between self-image and ideal self is compensation. The child who compensates is the 'goodie-good' child, the child who people-pleases or the child who puts enormous energy into certain tasks. The aim of compensation is to be perfect in order to please parents. By working so hard children reduce the possibility of failure and thus the possibility of withdrawal of love by parents. These children are hypersensitive to any hint of failure or criticism and can become extremely emotionally upset when things go against them or when they make a mistake. They react very badly to negative correction and find even positive correction difficult to take. These children are much more at risk than children who employ avoidance strategies. Because they put such tremendous effort into meeting the ideals set for them by parents, any failure by these children may result in feelings of hopelessness, cessation of any effort at all, withdrawal into a fantasy world or even the ultimate avoidance action of suicide. 'At least when I'm dead I can no longer fail or be hurt and rejected by others' is the hidden message behind many suicides.

Evidence of children using compensatory behaviours is all around us: perfectionism, extreme competitiveness, people-pleasing, high anxiety about examinations and so on. I recall a ten-year-old boy who was a compulsive hand-washer. His mother had always put great emphasis on cleanliness (ideal standard of behaviour set for child). When he was a baby she had washed him many times daily and, later on, demanded that the child wash his hands many times daily. The boy was now overcompensating in order to reduce any possibility of rejection by his mother for uncleanliness. The sad result was that his obsession with cleanliness led to extreme avoidance of situations where he might encounter dirt such as school, sport activities and outings with friends.

Children also compensate in the area of emotional responsiveness by, for example, smiling all the time and hiding their true feelings of hurt, anger or sadness.

⇨ Rebelliousness

Children who rebel are fighting back at parents who are the source of criticism and rejection. Rebelliousness may take on aspects of either avoidance or compensation. The child who reacts to his self-esteem dilemma by saying 'I could do it if I wanted to, but why should I do it to please you?' is both using avoidance and being rebellious. This tactic is clever because it shifts the focus onto the other by the verbal or physical attack, and it also means no effort is made so no failure can occur. I remember a fourteen-year-old adolescent who had been expelled from school because of verbal aggression towards certain teachers. As I got to know him better, it emerged that the teachers towards whom he was aggressive subconsciously reminded him of his father, who constantly criticised him and for whom he could never be good enough. The rebellious strategy worked. He got out of school and did not have to make any further academic efforts and so the possibility of rejection by his father was considerably lessened. In addition, the attention was on the teachers in the school who had had him expelled. What the boy needed most of all was his father's unconditional love and approval. It was revealing that the boy showed no aggression towards teachers who were kind and encouraging.

The second type of rebelliousness is that which accompanies compensation. Here the child maintains the extreme effort but adds the extra protection of rebelliousness in order to reduce the possibility of criticism. An example of this is where a child reacts with an emotional storm to any negative feedback. As a consequence, the parents learn not to say anything negative and so the strategy works. Of course, the real issue has not been resolved in that the gap between how the child sees himself and the ideals set down by parents remains. As long as this gap remains, the child will continue to use protective strategies as he is still emotionally at risk of rejection by parents.

⇨ Apathy

The problem here is different to that which leads to avoidance, compensation or rebelliousness; apathy results from the sad situation where the child – like the other troubled children – has a very poor self-image but in addition has no picture of an ideal self. The parents in such cases do not care enough to have any expectations of their children. You will recall that reasonable expectations are necessary for children to be motivated and challenged. Unreasonable expectations can have devastating effects, but having no expectations at all is even more destructive of children's mature development.

Apathy may result from overprotection, total neglect or emotionless caring. The overprotective parent does everything for the children and, unwittingly, sets no challenge for them. This parent also gives children a very poor self-image as they have no sense of being capable of doing things for themselves. Overprotection of children (or of adults!) is a gross act of neglect. It is perhaps easier to see that parents who are regularly abusive of their children – who do not care where they are, who they are with or whether they are safe and happy – are severely neglectful of their parenting responsibilities. Like overprotective parents, these parents do not set any ideals for their children. How could they when they rarely have any ideals or aspirations for their own personal development or for the couple relationship or family life? Children from such grossly neglectful homes, inevitably, have an extremely poor self-image. The poor self-image and the absence of ideals leads to apathetic behaviour. Apathy is extreme avoidance behaviour, its purpose being to reduce any further experiences of hurt and rejection.

I remember a thirteen-year-old girl who, when she came to me, had not been to school for seven months. She had been utterly 'spoilt' by both parents. When I asked her what she did all day she told me she got up at lunch time (her mother had her lunch ready) and for the rest of the day sat and watched television. The girl had absolutely no emotional, social, educational or career ambitions. I had to work at two levels with her in order to motivate her to act on her life: at the self-image level to give her a sense of her capability and at the ideal self level to give her a sense that there is a life out there to be seized and enjoyed. Involvement of the parents was crucial since they were reinforcing their daughter's helplessness through their own self-esteem difficulties.

■ Effects on parents

When parents send contradictory messages to each other, the effects can seriously damage the couple relationship and lead to the same kind of problems that children manifest: avoidance, compensation, rebelliousness and apathy. This simply reflects the fact that many of us as adults are still children – dependent on others for love and recognition and reactive when these needs are not met.

Individuals in a troubled couple relationship find ways to protect themselves from further hurt and rejection. These protective strategies are illustrated in the following couple inter-actions.

Protective strategy	Hidden message
Avoidance reactions	
• Being frequently absent from the home, particularly during critical decision-making times	• 'If I allow you to make all the decisions, will you now accept me?'
• Protecting oneself by with-drawal into drugs, alcohol, sleep, apathy, inattention, silence	• 'If I stay totally out of your way, will you now accept me?'
• Withdrawing through physical illness and helplessness	• 'If I'm sick and not able to cope, will you now take care of and love me?'
• Withdrawing into fantasy, delusions, hallucinations	• 'I can only find some recog-nition by being out of this world and away from you.' ➡

Compensation reactions	
• Constantly giving in to one's partner and withholding one's own opinions and needs	• 'If I agree with everything you say and do, will you now love and accept me?'
• Being the 'martyr' who carries all the responsibility of maintaining the relationship	• 'If I do everything for you, will you now love and accept me?'
• Overworking to earn enough money to meet all the demands of one's partner	• 'If I give you everything you want, will you now love and accept me?'
Rebellious reactions	
• Constantly arguing and fighting with one's partner	• 'I have to shout and fight my corner in order to be seen and valued by you.'
• Threatening to leave the relationship, return to mother or go off with somebody else	• 'I have to threaten you in order to find out whether or not you really want me.'
• Refusing to meet sexual and other needs of partner	• 'I want to be loved by you for myself and not for what I do.'
Apathetic reactions	
• Extreme withdrawal into inactivity and irresponsibility	• 'What's the point in trying as there is nothing I can do to get you to love me?'
• Frequently 'taking to the bed' or displaying feelings of deep depression and hopelessness	• 'I have lost all hope of ever getting you to love me'
• Total neglect of physical welfare, for example, gross undereating (anorexia nervosa), compulsive overeating (bulimia)	• 'I am starved of love in this relationship.'

Apathetic reactions occur when no behaviour on the part of the person impresses the other partner. It is a 'no win' situation and the consequences are extreme neglect of self, the couple relationship and, very often, the children.

The hidden messages reveal the real purpose of the protective strategies. However, because the real messages are unspoken, and because people tend to react literally to the overt verbal message, the problems in the relationship cannot be resolved by these strategies. The person on the receiving end is likely to see a partner's avoidance or rebelliousness as rejection and to see compensation as suffocation. Either way, she is likely to react by also employing a protective strategy. A vicious cycle of neglect and feelings of rejection is set in motion and both partners, unwittingly, contribute to the deterioration of the couple relationship. Because the relationship ceases to be unconditionally loving and supportive, and because the damaging interactions continue, the self-esteem of each partner is being continually adversely affected, individuality is being seriously blocked and, where there are children, their self-esteem and individuation process are also being affected.

❑ *Changing self-esteem within the family*

From the discussion above it is clear that the way family members relate to each other determines largely each member's self-esteem. The relationships within the family communicate messages regarding the lovability and capability of the members (self-image) and the standards of behaviour, personality characteristics and levels of performance that are expected of them (ideal self). Everyone in the family needs to ensure that all interactions are of a nature that elevate members' image of self and that create expectations which are realistic but also challenging.

Parents are the major influence here: their relationship with each other sets the tone for their relationship with the children, the children's relationship with them and the children's relationships with one another. It has already been pointed out that the strength of the couple relationship depends primarily on each partner's own relationship with self and the degree to which they have separated out from their family of origin.

Creating a loving and caring relationship with self – which is the hallmark of mature adulthood – is very similar to the process outlined below for the development of family inter-actions that elevate self-esteem. The only difference is that the mature adult, unlike the child, can care for herself independently of whether or not others care for her. The adult can learn to become the parent to self that her parents were unable to be, because of their own self-esteem problems. The child, of course, cannot do this and is totally dependent on parents for love and care. The process of individualising, whereby your sense of self no longer rests on the words and actions of others, is helped enormously by a supportive and unconditionally loving couple and family environment. The aspiration for children should be that they can stand apart from their parents and say: 'We can now independently feel good about ourselves; we feel confident and caring of ourselves; we can stand on our own two very capable feet.' The family is potentially the most fertile place for the development of each member's self-esteem.

▪ Essential tasks

When any one member of the family has a self-esteem problem, it is in the interest of all family members to help that person resolve her doubts about self. Many of the essential tasks involved in the development of the self-esteem of each member of the family have already been outlined:

- Unconditional loving (Chapter 4)
- Open expression of both welfare and emergency feelings (Chapter 7)
- Positive responsiveness to all expressed emotions (Chapter 7)
- Realistic fulfilment of needs for each member of the family (Chapter 6)
- Development of responsibility and fair sharing of tasks and resources among all family members (Chapter 9)
- Employment of direct and clear communication patterns between family members (Chapter 8)
- Creation of a family unit separate from parents' families of origin (Chapter 1)

■ Further tasks

Apart from these essential tasks, there are further tasks that are important in self-esteem development:

- Recognition of the rightness and goodness of each family member's body
- Affirmation of the unique social presence of each family member
- Affirmation of the limitless capability of each family member
- Encouragement of each family member to develop responsibly in ways unique to her
- Development of a healthy family lifestyle

⇨ Recognition of the rightness and goodness of each family member's body

There are few individuals who feel good about their bodies, have confidence in their own physical looks and take care of themselves in ways that indicate a deep valuing of and regard for their physical well-being. Many people rush and race, eat unhealthy foods, miss meals, eat on the run, overindulge in alcohol or other drugs, rarely rest and relax, fail to exercise and generally neglect their bodies. Your body carries your unique life-force, your limitless potential, your knowledge, skills, feelings and creativity – neglect it and you are liable to lose everything.

Many adults and children get negatively labelled because of certain bodily characteristics: size, shape, weight, skin texture, hair colour, absence of hair. Such labels as 'spotty', 'fatty', 'rat face', 'baldy', 'shortie', 'ladder', 'barrel' and 'rasher' can cause considerable pain to individuals and seriously damage their feelings about their physical selves. Comparisons with the physical appearance of others is another common way in which our physical self-image becomes negative. For many years I struggled with a rejection of my physical self due to experiences in early childhood, which were subsequently reinforced by myself and other adults insensitive to their 'cutting' remarks. Each member of the family needs to be affirmed for her own unique physical self. When a child is born I refuse to give in to the usual social pressure to answer the question 'who does he look like?' My answer is always that 'the child looks like himself'. The cosmetic industry has done much to damage the physical self-esteem of people and it is important that the family counter that force by celebrating equally the unique physical beauty of each member of the family. In my eyes each human being is a unique work of art never to be repeated in this universe.

⇝ Affirmation of the unique social presence of each family member

The family also needs to regularly affirm the unique social presence of each member. If the affirmation 'you are one of a kind and special' were a regular feature of family interactions what a boost to the self-esteem of the members that would be! Sadly, rather than affirming social uniqueness, families typically drown uniqueness under the tide of pressure towards conformity. Criticism, ridicule for difference and sarcasm for standing out from the crowd are frequent occurrences. Messages such as 'don't make a fool of yourself', 'don't be conspicuous' or 'don't get above yourself' all militate against family members developing an appreciation of the social uniqueness of each person. Yet, evidence of people's need to assert their difference is all around us. It is amazing what adults, adolescents and children find to make them stand out from the crowd – hair colour, hair style, 'way-out' clothes or expensive outfits, jewellery, 'eccentric' hobbies and interests, being with the 'right' people, achieving above the rest, winning competitions – all in order to be seen and recognised as different. Ironically, you are always different. No two humans are alike; each is unique, one of a kind, an unrepeatable phenomenon.

In developing individuality, family members need to know that they do not jeopardise acceptance and their place within the family. They need to be encouraged to celebrate their specialness. Comparisons sabotage such celebration. Some examples of comparisons that are often made between family members or with persons outside the family are:

- 'You're not a bit like my mother.' (husband to wife)
- 'Your cousins are more clever than you.' (parent to child)

- 'You should be more like your brother.' (parent to child)
- 'You'll never be as successful as my brother.' (wife to husband)

All such comparisons undermine the development of individuality and seriously undermine one's sense of uniqueness. Human beings have a deeply driven need to assert their uniqueness. The last thing a person wants is to be like somebody else. If family members are compelled to be like others (for example, children to be like parents or other siblings, or a parent to be like a neighbour or some colleague), they will develop little sense of individuality and will be highly dependent on others for recognition. Some family members drop out under extreme pressure to conform by, sadly, seeking the shadows and rarely showing the light of their own unique identity. The affirmation that needs to be sung loudly and often in the family is: each one of us is unique and special.

Parents need to be alert to the fact that children, particularly if they are insecure, can label one another in ways that deeply hurt each other's sense of uniqueness and specialness. This must not be tolerated and must be positively corrected whenever it occurs. Equally, parents need to model outward appreciation of each other's specialness.

➡ Affirmation of the limitless capability of each family member

Too often family members are told they are 'stupid', 'slow', 'lazy', 'average', 'bright' or 'very intelligent'. None of these labels is correct. Science has demonstrated that human beings only use 1 to 2 per cent of their brain cells and that they have limitless capability. Parents, teachers and children tend to confuse knowledge with intelligence. My own profession of psychology has done much to perpetuate that confusion by suggesting that so-called intelligence tests measure intelligence. Intelligence tests only measure knowledge and a limited range of knowledge at that. Indeed research has shown that intelligence tests are very poor predictors of academic or career development. In our culture a child who shows skill with a football is told 'you are good with your feet', or a child who is gifted mechanically is told 'you are good with your hands'. Only the child who shows academic ability is regarded as being 'good with the head'. However, all behaviour comes from the brain and it is wrong to identify academic ability with intelligence.

Differences emerging between children in their first days at school have to do with knowledge and skills and not with intelligence. Children come from different home and cultural backgrounds; some will have had the benefit of having experienced one-to-one conversations with parents, of being read to frequently, of a stimulating home environment, of an emphasis on love of learning and so on. These children will show higher knowledge levels than children who have not had such experiences; but the difference lies in experience not in capability.

It is essential that family members are frequently reminded of their limitless capacity to learn and that mistakes and failures are treated simply as indicators of present knowledge and skill levels and as opportunities for further learning. It is a sad reflection on our culture that only a tiny minority of children and adults have any sense of their wondrous capability. What most of us experience is a deep lack of confidence and a belief that many challenges are beyond us. The frequent affirmation within the family of each member's limitless capability gives a powerful boost to the process of individuation; its absence can lead to avoidance of challenge, over-anxiety, perfectionism, 'playing it safe', rebelliousness or apathy. Any of these reactions slows down or completely retards the development of the independence and individuality of each family member.

↬ Encouragement of each family member to develop responsibly in ways unique to her

You have seen in Chapters 2 and 3 how enmeshed or neglectful family relationships can seriously block the mature development of family members. Each family member has a right to her own unique growing and must not be forced down paths that deny that right. There are many parents who force their own ambitions on their children. I have worked with people who practised religious beliefs, held values and pursued study and career paths for which they actually had no inclination or liking. However, they felt compelled to comply as their spouses or parents would be either dreadfully disappointed or terribly angry and rejecting if they held contrary beliefs or pursued other paths. There are parents who want their children to have the educational and career opportunities they themselves did not have; they work hard with these 'unselfish' aims in mind and they genuinely believe they are doing it for the children's good. But, if the truth be told, they are doing it for themselves. The problem is that they forget to ask the children what it is that they want.

The uniqueness of family members could be affirmed by the encouragement of each to take up the ideas, interests, hobbies, studies, dress, beliefs, career and so on that 'fit' for them. This applies as much to parents as it does to children. Frequently, a spouse may attempt to block the development of a partner because the partner's ambitions are experienced as a threat. I have come across several men who ridiculed their female partner's wish to return to college or do personal development courses or return to work. Such sabotaging of growth and development can only result in a problematic relationship. Family members who are encouraged and supported in finding their own unique life-path retain a love of learning and of challenge; unfortunately, the converse is also true. If family members yield to the person in the family who dominates and controls how other members live their lives, there will be a tide of hidden resentment towards that person and a lack of self-fulfilment. When you live through another person's life how can you ever feel self-actualised?

Parents need to be observant of and attentive to the unique aspects of their own as well as their children's personalities:

- Their interests and hobbies
- Their special way of doing and seeing things
- Their way of caring for and helping others
- Their ways of resolving problems
- The people they like to be with
- The books, television programmes, music and academic subjects in which they show greatest interest

There is one sure thing about families: each member will find a way to be unique. Parents often say to me: 'How is it that John and Mary are like chalk and cheese even though they have been brought up in the same family environment?' The first reason is that no two children are ever brought up in the same way; the parents' own relationship is constantly changing and each parent relates to each child in different ways. But I believe there is also a deeper reason which is that the human psyche has an innate need to individualise itself. A child quickly spots at a subconscious level that 'to be like my brother or sister would mean I would not be seen for myself'. It is important that the child's (and the adult's) drive to express uniqueness is affirmed, celebrated and actively encouraged. Such a process sets family members up for a fulfilling life.

Responsibility lies at the heart of the expression of and the response to the uniqueness of family members. There is a difference between whims and fantasies, and genuine and responsible pursuit of one's own unique life goals. Family members cannot be allowed to avoid commitment and follow-through on ambitions; to do so would be an act of neglect.

➷ Development of a healthy family lifestyle

As has been said many times already, actions always speak louder than words. A healthy lifestyle is a mirror of the happy family. A healthy lifestyle means that the needs of the family are regularly and consistently met. Inevitably, the troubled family is neglectful of many essential needs. It requires consider-able discipline on the part of family members to create a balanced lifestyle. Time-management and planning are needed to ensure that most, if not all, of the family's essential needs are met within any one couple of days. Parents need to be particularly vigilant that they themselves model a balanced lifestyle and guide children into such responsible living.

Checklist of major family needs

- Emotional needs of love, affection, warmth, closeness, support, compassion, understanding, nurturance and humour

- Couple needs of time, space and resources to develop their emotional and sexual relationship   ➷

- Individual needs of each family member for own physical space, privacy, skills development, hobbies, interests, study, career, friendships and leisure
- Family needs for social outings, recreation, friendship, companionship and sharing of experiences, expertise and knowledge
- Physical needs of all family members of health, fitness, comfort, safety, food and warmth
- Sensual needs of all family members so that the five senses receive adequate stimulation
- Spiritual needs of transcendence, mystical experiences and meaningful explanation for existence

Responsiveness to these needs in a consistent, caring and active way is a major aspect of unconditional loving within a family. Dismissal of these responsibilities weakens the fabric of the family's well-being and the individuation process of each family member.

■ Family declaration of esteem

It may be useful for a family to have some means of reminding each other of the value and uniqueness of each and of the positive interactions that need to occur for the happy and healthy development of the family. The following declaration of esteem summarises many of the essential points outlined in this book. A frequent family reading of this declaration would serve not only to affirm each member but also to keep alive awareness of essential issues.

Family declaration of esteem

⊃ We respect, value, love and celebrate the uniqueness of each other. This uniqueness of each one of us is a matter of great joy and its enduring affirmation is the primary aim of this family.

⊃ The unique size, shape, height, skin type and hair colour of each of our bodies is accepted. We care for, nurture, exercise and rest our bodies and value every aspect of them. We do not compare our bodies to others and do not want our bodies to be like anybody else's.

→

⊃ We are aware of the mind's limitless capacity and allow each to manifest intelligence in ways that are unique to each one of us. We resist conformity that in any way blocks the unique development of any one of us.

⊃ We see mistakes and failures as opportunities for learning. Criticism, ridicule, scoldings, aggression and 'put-down' messages are not tolerated in this family.

⊃ We enjoy the achievements and successes of any one of us but do not hold on to any of them as indicators of worth. Our worth and value are independent of all of our actions.

⊃ We strongly distinguish between the being and the behaviour of each of us. We do not break relationships with each other because of a 'bit' of unacceptable behaviour.

⊃ We are unconditionally loving of each other.

⊃ We are firm on responsibilities and because we love each other we do not allow each other to slide out of responsibility. No action on the part of any one of us takes away from the worth, value and uniqueness of each of us.

⊃ We encourage each other to own and take responsibility for our thoughts, images, ambitions, words and actions, whether they be of a positive or negative nature and whether they be towards each other or self.

⊃ We recognise there are things we have done or may do that we regret or will regret but we are determined to grow from these experiences and learn to love self and each other more deeply every day.

⊃ We encourage each other to be honest, direct and open about behaviours that are distressful to each other but in ways that do not hurt each other. We will take responsibility and healing action for any neglect or hurt we may have caused.

⊃ No matter what happens we will not cease to care for each other.

⊃ Each one of us has immense ability to grow and develop in this world. We encourage each other to be independent, to stand on our own feet, to live and determine our own life-path and to leave the family, when ready, to further pursue our own goals in life.

CHAPTER 11

Leaving the Family

- ❑ *Leaving is an act of love*
- ❑ *Those who dare not leave*
- ❑ *What leaving means*

*The degree to which I can create relationships which
facilitate the growth of others as separate persons
is a measure of the growth I have
achieved in myself.*
Carl R. Rogers

❑ *Leaving is an act of love*

In the first chapter it was stated that the purpose of the family
is the optimum development of each of its members. Optimum
development means that each person is brought to emotional
independence and to a belief in one's capacity to care for
oneself. The leavetaking of the family is not necessarily a
physical exodus, even though this is advisable for young adult
family members. As an adult it is difficult to establish one's
own life space and pattern while living under the roof of other
adults (mostly parents or in-laws).

I have come across many young couples who moved in either
to his or to her parents' home and later experienced great difficulties in these two-generation families. Take, for example, a
young woman moving in to her husband's home. She may feel
that the place is not her own, the young couple may have difficulties in establishing their own private space, and their
sexual life may be hampered by the sense of the 'walls having
ears'. Likewise, her in-laws may have difficulty in adjusting to
the situation and feel that their taste in decoration, their ways
of living and their opinions are being judged by their daughter-
in-law. This is a very difficult mix and both the parents and the

young couple would need considerable maturity and separateness to work out the clear boundaries needed between the two couple relationships. Matters become even more complicated when there are other young adult offspring in the house. Further difficulties arise when the young couple begin to have their own family. Young couples need all the advantages possible when starting to live together. The first two years of any couple relationship are the most difficult while the partners are adjusting to the differences between them. The old saying 'love is blind but marriage is an eye-opener' holds a lot of wisdom.

For a young couple physical separateness from families of origin is important. However, emotional separateness from family of origin (whether living in or away from home) is a far more important issue. Unless this emotional separateness is established, a young adult will have major difficulties leaving home. Of course, when young adult members of a family have difficulties leaving home, this mirrors the parents' emotional dependence on their offspring. Somehow, in these families the parents did not nurture independence in their children. These parents continue to live their lives through their children and in doing so they block their own and their children's emotional independence, self-belief and self-reliance. Ironically, it is the parents who encourage independence who maintain strong bonds with their adult offspring for the duration of their lives. Those who foster dependence may keep their adult children tied to them but the relationship will harbour resentment, guilt, anger and blame. People have told me of great tides of anger towards parents who either dominated or manipulated them into always being there for them. These trapped children, ranging from twenty to sixty years of age, dare not have lives of their own, and are told they are selfish when they attempt to break away. Consequently, serious emotional storms, including rage, threats, accusations, violence and suicide threats, can occur when a member attempts to leave an unhappy family.

I recall one woman in her thirties whose mother completely dominated her. The mother had not approved of any man she brought across the threshold. At one stage the daughter had been having a clandestine relationship and when its existence was discovered by the mother, conflict erupted. Somehow the daughter found the courage to say 'whether you like him or not I'm going to marry him'. Her mother then had a heart attack. Great drama ensued: arrival of ambulance, admission to coronary care unit, consternation in the family. The mother was released a week later, fine and healthy. The daughter did not raise the issue of her lover anymore until she came for therapy. In the course of therapy she became aware that she was not responsible for her mother; it was not she who caused her mother to have the hysterical heart attack but her mother herself. It was the mother's dependence and dominant behaviour, her father's passivity, and her own collusion with these behaviours that led to her lack of decisiveness and lack of independence at this stage of her life. The goals of therapy were to help her to respect and value her own needs, values and ambitions, to break the dependent relationship with her mother and to create more adult–adult relationships with both her parents. Eventually she married the 'unworthy' man, not heeding her mother's disapproval.

The major tasks for parents are to:

- Promote independence in themselves and in their children
- Let go of children once they reach late adolescence
- Take responsibility for their own lives and promote responsibility for themselves in their offspring
- Create adult–adult relationships with their adolescent and adult offspring

Parents often resist the suggestion that they should stop parenting children who are in late adolescence or young adulthood. At that stage it is important to begin to develop more of an adult–adult than child–parent relationship. This comes more easily to parents who have developed their own independence. Parents can lift what can become an intolerable burden – themselves – from their children's shoulders when they let their children know that they are quite capable of taking responsibility for their own lives. Parents need to let their children know that what they want is an enduring friendship with them and the thrill of seeing them set up their own independent lives. In supporting and encouraging their children's emotional leavetaking, and eventually their physical departure, parents are truly loving their children. The rewards for parents who follow this path are great: an enduring mature relationship with their children for the rest of their lives; and the comfort and security of knowing that, as parents, they have achieved what is best for themselves and for their children.

There are individuals who physically leave the family – may even move to another country – but there still has not been an emotional leavetaking. Some people leave home through rebellion against families that were overprotective or neglectful. Unfortunately, they in turn have rejected or become conditional with their parents. Furthermore, since they have not become emotionally independent they will continue to seek the approval and respect of others or else be dismissive of others and become isolated or loners. People who 'people-please' subconsciously seek to cast others as substitute parents and, likewise, adults who put on a tough veneer and pretend they need no one are showing deep dependence. As human beings we have many needs which can be met only in relationships with others. However, having needs is not dependence. When you acknowledge your needs, take responsibility for them and express them in a way that allows the other person the freedom to say 'yes' or 'no', you are being truly independent. When you demand that people meet your needs or when you act as if you do not need anybody, you are showing dependence.

❏ *Those who dare not leave*

It is not difficult to recognise the kind of people who remain enmeshed with their families and have difficulties in becoming autonomous. Dependence may be manifested through:

* overcontrol indicators, or
* undercontrol indicators.

Overcontrol indicators of dependence refer to behaviours that 'hold in' the hidden conflicts arising from low self-esteem, the need for approval from parents, the unrealistic expectations of parents, conditional or neglectful parenting and fears of life. Undercontrol indicators spring from the same sources but the vulnerability is manifested in this case through behaviours that 'let out' the rage and frustration within. Though the inability to love and leave the family may manifest itself in these very different ways, the underlying cause always lies in either a conditional or neglectful family of origin. Unfortunately, many of these adults who fail to love and leave the family go on to re-create the very relationships that have brought them so much pain, hurt and dependence.

Overcontrol characteristics of adults who do not love and leave the family

- Having middle to poor self-esteem
- Being childish and dependent when in parents' company
- Still living at home beyond early to mid-twenties
- Being timid and fearful
- Conforming to values, morals, beliefs and wishes of parents and others
- People-pleasing
- Being shy, reserved, quiet and passive
- Being manipulative
- Lacking in confidence
- Avoiding challenges and responsibilities
- Being insecure in social and novel situations
- Being fearful of mistakes and failures
- Being unable to say 'no' to parents and others
- Taking responsibility for parents' well-being
- Failing to confront on unacceptable behaviour for the sake of 'peace and quiet'
- Failing to establish own independent home
- Allowing interference with or intrusion into the family by others (whether single, couple or family situation)
- Looking for approval from parents and others
- Clinging to parents or friends
- Though living away, visiting or phoning home frequently

➡

- Being indecisive
- Wanting to prove oneself to parents and others
- Never or rarely visiting parents
- Withdrawing when visiting parents
- Finding it difficult to create relationships with others
- Being isolated and lonely
- Lacking ambition
- Being perfectionist
- Being overambitious
- Worrying all the time
- Constantly putting others' needs before own
- Not participating in group discussions
- Being dependent on opinions and views of parents and others
- Being overconscientious
- Day-dreaming
- Sulking and maintaining silences
- Rarely asking for anything for self
- Frequently feeling guilty
- Being dependent on prescribed drugs, alcohol or illicit drugs
- Being dependent on appearances, success, physical looks etc.
- Being hypersensitive to criticism
- Suffering psychosomatic complaints (for example, headaches, back pain, arthritis, chest pains, stomach problems)
- Being phobic (for example, claustrophobic or agoraphobic)
- Being fearful of making a fool of oneself
- Having an unhealthy lifestyle
- Compulsively checking, cleaning, time-keeping etc.
- Believing that all others cope much better with life
- Frequently feeling depressed and hopeless
- Having suicidal thoughts or making suicide attempts
- Being in the habit of putting oneself down

Any one of these indicators reveals some level of dependence; the more of the list that applies to a person, the greater the level of dependence. The intensity and frequency of occurrence of such experiences are also important in determining the level of dependence.

Undercontrol characteristics of adults who do not love and leave the family

- Having middle to low self-esteem
- Still living at home beyond early to mid-twenties
- Blaming parents and others for personal vulnerability
- Being aggressive, dominant and narcissistic in relationships
- Being irresponsible
- Being boastful
- Attention-seeking
- Being a spendthrift
- Being possessive and controlling in relationships
- Being loud in social situations
- Denying lack of confidence or denying any problems
- Being dismissive of other people's needs
- Being overdemanding
- Being overambitious
- Being extremely competitive with others
- Attacking and abusing others who disagree
- Rarely if ever going to see parents
- Being hostile when visiting parents
- Being irritable, moody and volatile
- Being violent
- Not listening to others
- Having difficulty in creating relationships
- Constantly needing to be in another's company
- Neglecting personal, physical and safety needs
- Drinking alcohol heavily
- Gambling compulsively   ➥

- Being critical and ridiculing of others
- Being cynical and sarcastic
- Acting out by hurting oneself (for example, banging fist off solid object, cutting oneself, drug over-dosing)
- Damaging other people's property
- Overworking
- Being argumentative
- Frequently crying
- Stealing
- Having difficulties in concentration
- Being uncooperative
- Being unable to take criticism (whether positive or negative)
- Frequently asking for help or reassurance
- Avoiding many responsibilities
- Frequently missing work

What many people fail to recognise is that in not leaving home and failing to become emotionally independent, not only are they not loving themselves but neither are they loving their parents. Adults who remain in their home of origin often rationalise their dependent behaviour with such statements as:

- 'They (parents) couldn't do without me.'
- 'My mother would have no life if I left.'
- 'My duty is to look after them.'
- 'They wouldn't hear of or accept my leaving.'
- 'What would people say if I left?'
- 'I'd feel guilty if I left.'

When you examine these statements you see that they completely dismiss the capacity of parents to look after themselves. Protection is an act of neglect; it serves only to maintain and exacerbate the vulnerability of the parents who are protected. This is hardly an act of love! Unconditional loving shows belief in others' capability to care for themselves. It is good to remember that our parents existed and managed without us before we were born. But there is a deeper issue underlying these statements and that is the person's own doubts about himself. In 'staying on for the parents' sake', the person has found a protection against having to take responsibility for his own life and leavetaking from home. In becoming independent and leaving the family, the person is showing love of self and love of parents. In staying, the person neglects both.

❏ *What leaving means*

The frequency with which one encounters the overcontrol and undercontrol manifestations of dependence gives some measure of how few families achieve the goals of independence and mature leavetaking of the family. Obviously the degree of failure varies from family to family. The greater the neglect or conditionality within the family, the greater the level of non-separation and dependence shown by that family's members. Once young adults become aware of this dependence, they have a responsibility to separate out from their families of origin and create their own independent life-paths. If they manage this, the cycle of neglect will stop and in their future relationships with partner or spouse, and later with children, they will pass on their hard-earned maturity.

My own experience of working with people in late adolescence or young adulthood is that when there is cooperation and support from parents, the young person can fairly quickly achieve independence and develop a more mature relationship with parents. However, if parents do not cooperate and continue to try to control their adult offspring, the process is made considerably more difficult. Generally speaking, once parents are gently made aware of what needs to happen – as much for themselves as for their adult offspring – they do cooperate. There are some parents who need a lot of individual help before they are ready to 'release' their offspring and, unfortunately, many are reluctant to seek that help. Nevertheless, whether or not I get the cooperation of parents, I do my utmost to help young adults to separate out from home. I help them to see their parents' deep dependence and low self-esteem and to develop a feeling of love and compassion for them but also to see that the process of loving and leaving the family needs to be carried through to its conclusion of independence and an unconditional and mature relationship with parents. When parents cannot accept this process, I encourage young people to hold the door of unconditional acceptance open, but to firmly continue their own emancipation.

In the case of an adult, the means of establishing self-reliance, independence of family of origin and mature relationships with parents are the same as those outlined in earlier chapters for the creation of a happy family. The one difference is that rather than relying on parents and other family members for a sense of self and independence, as an adult you now learn to rely and depend on yourself. Basically, you need to parent yourself in a way that fosters high self-esteem, a belief in your own immense capability and a deep and unconditional loving and acceptance of yourself and of others. The characteristics to aim for are outlined below.

Characteristics of adults who love and leave the family

- Having high self-esteem
- Unconditionally loving and valuing yourself, parents and other family members
- Seeing parents as persons in their own right
- Seeing yourself as a person in your own right
- Being caring of self, parents and other family members
- Believing that parents and other family members can take responsibility for their own lives
- Respecting beliefs, values, morals, religious affiliation and opinions of parents and other family members
- Respecting your own beliefs, values, morals, religious affiliation and opinions
- Resisting imposition by parents or other family members of their beliefs, values, morals, religious affiliation and opinions
- Not imposing your own beliefs, values, morals, religious affiliation and opinions on others

➥

- Not conforming to parents' and society's expectations of what you 'ought' to be
- Being self-directing, independent and self-responsible
- Seeking out challenges in order to explore your own potential
- Being open to change
- Being spontaneous in expression of feelings, ambitions, wishes and values
- Being accurate in appraisal of reality
- Acknowledging strengths and weaknesses
- Being fair and just
- Enjoying privacy
- Loving life
- Being spiritual
- Being caring of the environment
- Having a healthy lifestyle
- Being creative
- Being decisive
- Competing with self not with others
- Creating independent intimate relationships with a few significant others
- Being able to say 'no' to self, parents, other family members and others
- Positively helping when parents are unable to do things for themselves
- Not permitting interference and intrusion by parents or others into your own life, home and family
- Communicating directly and clearly
- Owning your own feelings, dreams, wishes, needs, ambitions
- Asking for help, reassurance, support, advice and comfort when needed
- Respecting the other person's right to say 'yes' or 'no' to your expressed needs
- Seeing mistakes and failures as opportunities for learning

The family then is the nest from which offspring fly in order to create their own independent existence and, later on, if they so choose, to bring this independence and separateness into the creation of new couple and family relationships. These offspring maintain close, affectionate, supportive and caring relationships with their parents but do not take responsibility for their parents' lives. If parents become disabled in later years, they give as much help as possible and they give that help wholeheartedly. The person who loves and leaves the family in the positive ways described above has a true and enduring unconditional love for self, parents, brothers and sisters and others.

Bass, Ellen and Laura Davis, *The Courage to Heal*, Mandarin Paperbacks, 1990

Beattie, Melody, *Codependent No More*, Hazelden, 1987

Bradshaw, John, *Homecoming*, London: Judy Piatkas (Publishers), 1993

Briggs, Dorothy Corkille, *Your Child's Self-Esteem*, New York: Doubleday, 1967

Briggs, Dorothy Corkille, *Celebrate Your Self*, New York: Doubleday, 1977

Clarke, Jean Illsley, *Self-Esteem: A Family Affair*, New York: Harper and Row, 1978

Curran, Dolores, *Traits of a Healthy Family*, New York: Ballantine Books, 1983

Dobson, Fitzgerald, *How to Discipline with Love*, New York: Rawson Associates, 1977

Dreikurs, Rudolf, *Happy Children*, London: Fontana/Collins, 1982

Friday, Nancy, *My Mother, My Self*, London: Fontana/Collins, 1979

Gordon, Thomas, *P. E. T.*, London: New American Library, 1975

Gupta, Rajinder M. and Peter Coxhead (eds.), *Intervention with Children*, London: Routledge, 1990

Haley, Jay and Lynn Hoftman, *Techniques of Family Therapy*, New York: Basic Books, 1967

Hay, Louise L., *You Can Heal Your Life*, London: Eden Grove Editions, 1984

Humphreys, Tony, *A Different Kind of Teacher*, Dublin: Gill & Macmillan, 1996

Humphreys, Tony, *The Power of 'Negative' Thinking*, Dublin: Gill & Macmillan, 1996

Humphreys, Tony, *Self-Esteem: The Key to Your Child's Education*, Dublin: Gill & Macmillan, 1996

Kopp, Sheldon, *All God's Children are Lost But Only a Few Can Play the Piano*, London: Aquarian/Thorsons, 1991

Laing, R. D., *The Voice of Experience*, Harmondsworth: Penguin Books, 1983

Lerner, Harriet Goldhor, *The Dance of Anger*, London: Grapevine, 1990

Lieberman, Mendel and Marion Hardie, *Resolving Family and Other Conflicts*, Santa Cruz: Unity Press, 1981

Madanes, Cloe, *Strategic Family Therapy*, Oxford: Jossey-Bass Publishers, 1991

McKay, Matthew and Patrick Fanning, *Self-Esteem*, Oakland, California: New Harbinger Publications, 1987

Miller, Alice, *The Drama of Being a Child*, London: Virago Press, 1988

Peck, M. Scott, *The Road Less Travelled*, Century Paperback Series, 1987

Satir, Virginia, *Peoplemaking*, Palo Alto, California: Science and Behaviour Books, 1972

Satir, Virginia, *Conjoint Family Therapy*, London: Souvenir Press, 1980

Satir, Virginia, *The New Peoplemaking*, Palo Alto, California: Science and Behaviour Books, 1988

Scott, Gini Graham, *Resolving Conflict*, Oakland, California: New Harbinger Publications, 1990

Siegel, Bernie, *Peace, Love and Healing*, London: Rider, 1990

Simonton, Stephanie Matthews, *The Healing Family*, London: Bantam Books, 1988

Skynner, Robin and John Cleese, *Families and How to Survive Them*, London: Methuen, 1984

Smith, Manuel J., *When I Say No I Feel Guilty*, London: Bantam Books, 1981

Walrond-Skinner, Sue (ed.), *Family and Marital Psychotherapy*, London: Routledge and Kegan Paul, 1979

Walrond-Skinner, Sue, *Family Therapy*, London: Routledge and Kegan Paul, 1986

Wolff, Sula, *Children Under Stress*, Harmondsworth: Penguin Books, 1981